W9-ANR-253

THE GREAT BOOK OF
STATES

J. P. Allice

Publications International, Ltd.

J. P. Allice specializes in nonfiction for young people. She is the author of eight books and more than one hundred magazine articles.

Factual verification: Suzanne Northington

PICTURE CREDITS:

FRONT COVER: iStockphoto; Photodisc; Shutterstock; Thinkstock

BACK COVER: iStockphoto; Photodisc

Alamy Images: Daniel Dempster Photography, 73 (bottom right); Clint Farlinger, 43 (top); jaxpix, 15 (bottom); David Lyons, 13 (top right); William Manning, 41 (bottom); Buddy Mays, 67 (top); North Wind Picture Archives, 8 (bottom left), 72 (left), 78 (bottom); Prisma/Newman Mark, 22 (bottom); PVstock.com, 41 (top); RWP, 61 (bottom); Philip Scalia, 23 (top); Michael Snell, 45 (bottom right); **AP Images:** 8 (bottom right), 11 (top center), 23 (center), 34 (bottom left), 51 (top), 65 (bottom left center & bottom right), 73 (bottom left), 77 (top & left center), 78 (left center), 99 (bottom left), 105 (right center), 121 (top right & right center), 122 (center); **Art Explosion:** 103 (top); **Artville:** 120 (center); **Colleen Briedrick:** 115 (center), 125 (center); **Corbis:** Harris Barnes/AgStock Images, 77 (bottom); Tom Bean, 43 (bottom); Annie Griffiths Belt, 55 (top); Richard Cummins, 9 (top right); Franz-Marc Frei, 55 (bottom); Bob Krist, 81 (top right); Danny Lehman, 95 (bottom right); Francis G. Mayer, 7 (right center); David Muench, 53 (center), 118 (bottom); Tom Nebbia, 28 (bottom); Louie Psihoyos, 67 (bottom right); **Dustin Drase:** 41 (top right); **Dreamstime:** 109 (bottom left), 119 (bottom left), 127 (right center); **Ford Motor Company:** 46 (left & right); **Getty Images:** 87 (top), 99 (bottom center); AFP (bottom right); De Agostini Picture Library, 29 (bottom right); Time Life Pictures, 65 (center), 121 (left center); **iStockphoto:** 11 (center), 17 (top left), 42 (bottom), 49 (bottom left), 51 (bottom left & bottom right), 63 (top), 76 (bottom top right), 98 (center), 119 (top); **Latham Jenkins/CircumerroStock.com:** 17 (bottom); **Jupiterimages:** 16 (center), 80 (top left), 96 (left center); **Library of Congress:** 11 (top left), 13 (top left, top left center, bottom left, bottom left center & bottom right center), 22 (left center), 24 (bottom left), 27 (left center, bottom left & right center), 28 (center), 29 (top right), 31 (top), 34 (top), 35 (top right center), 38 (bottom), 39 (right center), 40 (bottom right), 41 (top left), 45 (left), 52 (bottom), 54 (bottom left & bottom right), 61 (center), 63 (right center), 65 (top, bottom left, bottom right center, 69 (top left), 70 (top right, top right center, bottom left, bottom right center, bottom right), 71 (top), 76 (left center), 77 (left & right center), 79 (top), 80 (bottom), 84 (left), 86 (right center), 94 (left), 101 (left center), 105 (top), 106 (bottom), 113 (top), 120 (top right); **Media Bakery:** 59 (top), 121 (bottom); **Doug Mitchel:** 39 (top); **S.J. Morrow:** 59 (center); **NASA:** 41 (top right center), 57 (left center & right center), 65 (bottom far left), 121 (top center); **Photodisc:** 90 (bottom), 115 (top), 117 (bottom left), 124 (bottom); **Photos To Go:** 120 (bottom); **PIL Collection:** 33 (top), 41 (bottom right center & bottom right), 45 (bottom), 65 (bottom far right), 70 (left center & bottom left center); **Public Domain:** 13 (top right center), 45 (top right); **Russian Federation:** 11 (top right); **Shutterstock:** title page, contents, 7 (top left & bottom right), 10 (center), 11 (bottom left & bottom right), 13 (left center & right center), 16 (top), 17 (top right), 18 (right center & bottom), 19 (center & bottom), 21 (top, right center, center & bottom), 24 (top & bottom right), 25 (top left, top center & top right), 26 (center & bottom), 27 (top left, top center & top right), 30 (center), 31 (center & bottom), 32 (top), 33 (center), 35 (top left, top right & bottom right), 37 (bottom left), 38 (center), 40 (top & bottom left), 42 (center), 43 (left center & right center), 44 (left), 47 (top & bottom), 48 (center & bottom), 49 (top left, top left center, center, bottom center & bottom right), 50 (left), 54 (right center), 56 (center & bottom), 60 (left & right), 63 (left center), 64 (center & bottom), 67 (center & bottom left), 68 (top, left center, right center & bottom), 69 (left center, center & top right), 70 (center), 71 (left center & right center), 73 (top left), 74 (left), 75 (top left, top center, top right & bottom left), 76 (bottom right), 77 (right), 79 (bottom), 81 (bottom), 83 (bottom left & bottom right), 85 (center), 86 (left center & bottom), 87 (bottom), 89 (top), 90 (left center), 91 (top left & top right), 93 (left), 95 (top & bottom left), 96 (bottom), 97 (left center), 98 (bottom), 99 (top left center, top center, top right center & top right), 101 (top, right center & bottom), 102 (bottom left), 103 (top, left center & right center), 104 (top left, left center, right center & bottom), 107 (top right, right center, bottom left, bottom left center & bottom right center), 108 (left & bottom), 109 (top left, top right, bottom left center, & bottom center), 110 (left center), 111 (top, left, left center, center, bottom left, right, right center & bottom right), 112 (center), 113 (center & bottom), 115 (left center & bottom), 116 (center), 117 (top, left, left center, center, right, bottom center & bottom right), 118 (center), 119 (left center, center, right center & bottom right), 120 (top left), 121 (center), 122 (bottom), 123 (bottom), 126 (bottom), 127 (top right, left center & bottom); **Smithsonian Institution:** 58 (bottom); **SuperStock:** 54 (left center), 59 (bottom), 82 (left), 110 (bottom), 121 (top left); age fotostock, 73 (top right), 112 (bottom); Lee Canfield, 125 (top); Larry Chiger, 63 (bottom); Everett Collection, 12 (bottom); IndexStock, 16 (bottom); JTB Photo, 99 (center); Lonely Planet, 79 (right center); Newberry Library, 83 (top); **Thinkstock:** contents, 7 (center), 8 (center), 12 (top), 14 (left), 15 (top left & center), 17 (center), 18 (left center), 22 (right center), 24, 25 (bottom), 29 (top left), 30 (bottom), 32 (bottom left & bottom right), 33 (bottom), 34 (bottom right), 37 (top left, center & top right), 39 (left center), 44 (bottom), 47 (center), 49 (top right & top right center), 50 (bottom), 52 (center), 53 (top & bottom), 54 (top), 55 (center), 57 (bottom), 58 (center), 61 (top), 75 (bottom right), 76 (center), 83 (center), 85 (bottom), 89 (center & bottom), 93 (bottom), 98 (center), 99 (top left), 103 (bottom), 105 (left center), 107 (top left, top center, top right center & bottom), 109 (bottom right center & bottom right), 110 (center), 116 (bottom), 123 (top left & top right), 127 (top left, top center & center); **United States Army:** 66 (bottom); **United States Federal Government:** 67 (bottom center), 70 (top left); **White Eagle Studio:** 41 (bottom left); 66 (center)

Contributing illustrators: Ralph S. Canaday; Sue Carlson; Drew-Brook-Cormack Associates; Brian Fyffe

Flag illustrations: Robesus

Louis Weber, CEO
Publications International, Ltd.
7373 North Cicero Avenue
Lincolnwood, Illinois 60712

ISBN-13: 978-1-4508-2178-0
ISBN-10: 1-4508-2178-2

Manufactured in China.

8 7 6 5 4 3 2 1

Library of Congress Control Number: 2011920084

Contents

The United States of America

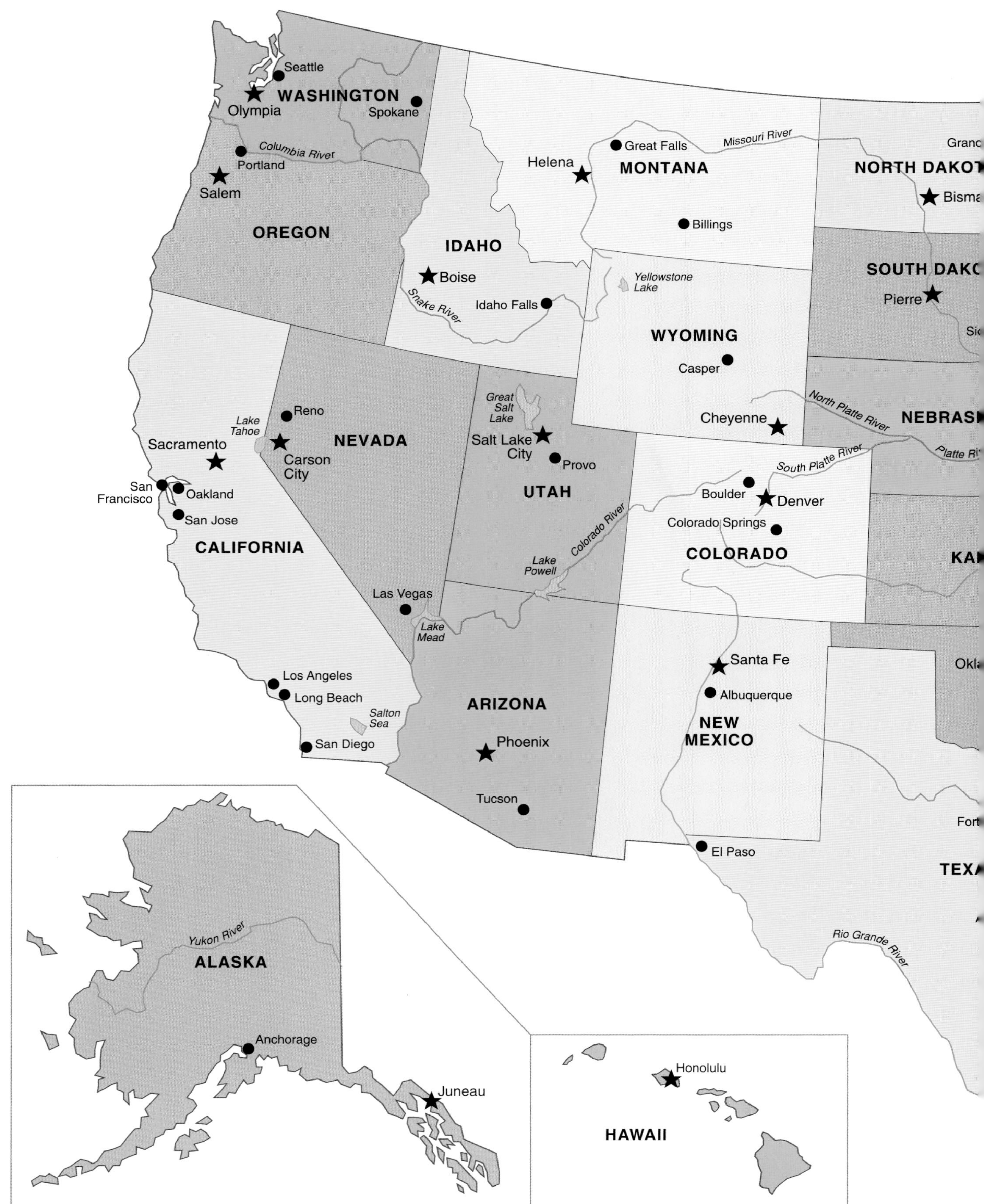

Lake of the Woods
Isle Royale
Lake Superior
NESOTA
St. Paul
nneapolis
Mississippi River
WISCONSIN
Green Bay
Milwaukee
Madison
Lake Michigan
MICHIGAN
Lake Huron
Lansing
Detroit
Lake Ontario
Lake Erie
NEW HAMPSHIRE
MAINE
VERMONT
Lake Champlain
Augusta
Montpelier
Portland
Concord
Connecticut River
NEW YORK
MASSACHUSETTS
Boston
Syracuse
Albany
Providence
Buffalo
Hartford
RHODE ISLAND
CONNECTICUT
Long Island
PENNSYLVANIA
Newark
New York
IOWA
Cedar Rapids
Des Moines
Chicago
Cleveland
Philadelphia
Trenton
Harrisburg
Pittsburg
NEW JERSEY
Dover
Baltimore
Annapolis
OHIO
Columbus
ILLINOIS
Wabash River
INDIANA
Springfield
Indianapolis
Cincinnati
Ohio River
WEST VIRGINIA
Washington, DC
DELAWARE
MARYLAND
MISSOURI
VIRGINIA
Kansas City
St. Louis
Jefferson City
Louisville
Frankfort
Charleston
Richmond
Norfolk
Virginia Beach
KENTUCKY
Raleigh
NORTH CAROLINA
Nashville
Charlotte
Tulsa
ARKANSAS
TENNESSEE
Tennessee River
Arkansas River
Mississippi River
Memphis
Columbia
Atlanta
Savannah River
SOUTH CAROLINA
Little Rock
Birmingham
Charleston
MISSISSIPPI
ALABAMA
GEORGIA
Jackson
Montgomery
LOUISIANA
Mobile
Tallahassee
Jacksonville
FLORIDA
Baton Rouge
Orlando
Houston
New Orleans
Tampa
St. Petersburg
Lake Okeechobee
Miami
Florida Keys

New England

The roots of the United States are in New England. This is the land where the Pilgrims and Puritans lived almost 400 years ago. It is also where the Revolutionary War began, when the people of the colonies rose up to fight for their independence. The six states of the New England region are in the northeastern part of the country. They are full of historic sites and beauty.

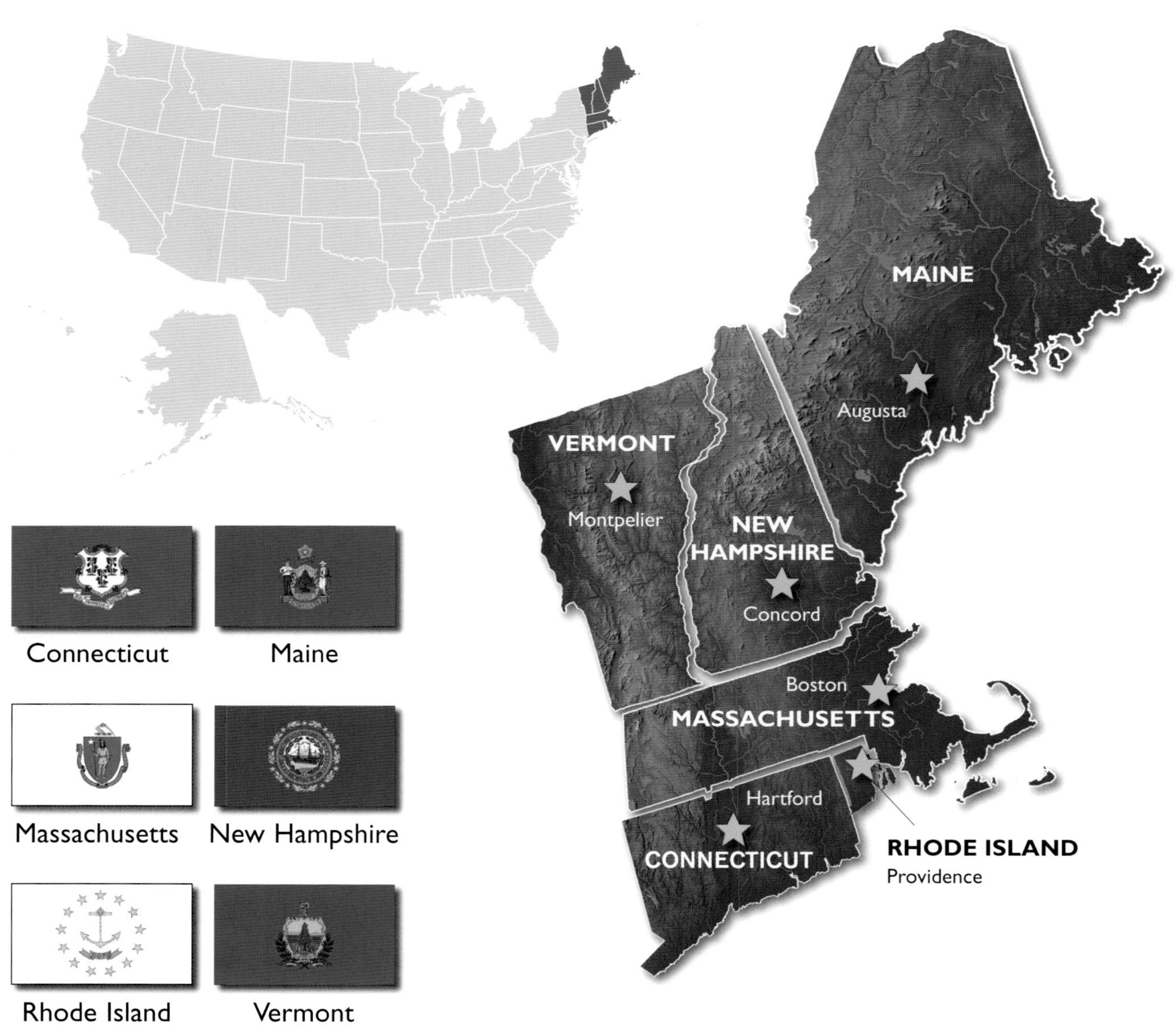

The Nature of New England

There are many things to do outdoors in New England. In the winter, you can ski in the mountains or play in the deep snow. In the spring, it gets very wet. New Englanders call it the mud season. You can watch the birds fly north in the spring and see the trees in blossom. In the summer, you can boat, swim, or explore the rocky beaches. In the fall, you can jump in piles of yellow, orange, and red leaves. New England is known for a beautiful fall because of all the amazing, colorful leaves on the trees.

Ice That Moved Land

The states of New England share many of the same land features. Many of the shores are full of rocky bays and inlets. Rugged mountains cover much of the land, especially in the north. Geologists (scientists who study the earth) think that these landforms were made by glaciers. Glaciers are large bodies of slow-moving ice. During the last ice age many thousands of years ago, glaciers moved over the land to form the beautiful scenery we see today.

To Join or Not to Join...

The states of New England were among the first colonies of the New World. But after many years as colonies, they did not want to be ruled by Great Britain. The people fought for their freedom. When the Revolutionary War was over, not all of the New England colonies joined the United States right away. Which ones did not join right away? Maine and Vermont did not join. Vermont became a state in 1791, and Maine became a state in 1820.

A National Park of Islands

Acadia National Park is a national park in New England. It is a park made up of many islands. It is located along the rocky coast of Maine. The woods here are filled with all kinds of wild plants and animals. The tallest mountain on the Atlantic coast, called Cadillac Mountain, stands in this park. Visitors can go to the ocean, hike the woods, or climb some of the mountains. A favorite place for people to see in Acadia Park is Thunderhole, where the cliffs meet the ocean. When the waves hit the cliffs, it really does sound like thunder!

Connecticut

Connecticut is the third smallest state, but don't let its size fool you! It has always been a state that has helped others. During the Revolutionary War, people from Connecticut gave the Continental Army guns, meat, and flour. Today, people work in factories making aircraft parts, helicopters, and submarines. George Washington once called Connecticut the "Provision State" (provision means to give something that is needed), and this state has lived up to that name.

STATE FACTS

Statehood: January 9, 1788—5th state
Capital: Hartford
Nickname: The Constitution State
Motto: He Who Transplanted Still Sustains
State Bird: American robin
State Flower: Mountain laurel

Connecticut's Home

Connecticut sits between the large state of New York and the tiny state of Rhode Island. The northern part of Connecticut has hills and small mountains. The southern shore of Connecticut is next to the Atlantic Ocean. This part of the Atlantic Ocean is called Long Island Sound. Fish, crabs, oysters, and scallops live in Long Island Sound. If you're on the shore, you will see birds, turtles, and maybe even a harbor seal!

Connecticut's State Heroes

Nathan Hale

Hale was a teacher who became a spy during the Revolutionary War. He helped George Washington. He was caught and hanged by the British without a trial.

Prudence Crandall

Prudence Crandall taught African American girls at her school, even though she faced danger for doing that.

Fourth-graders from Bristol, Connecticut

These students were upset! They realized the state capitol had a statue of Hale but not of Crandall. They wrote letters and raised money until a statue was made for Crandall.

Students unveil the statue of Prudence Crandall at the Connecticut Capitol.

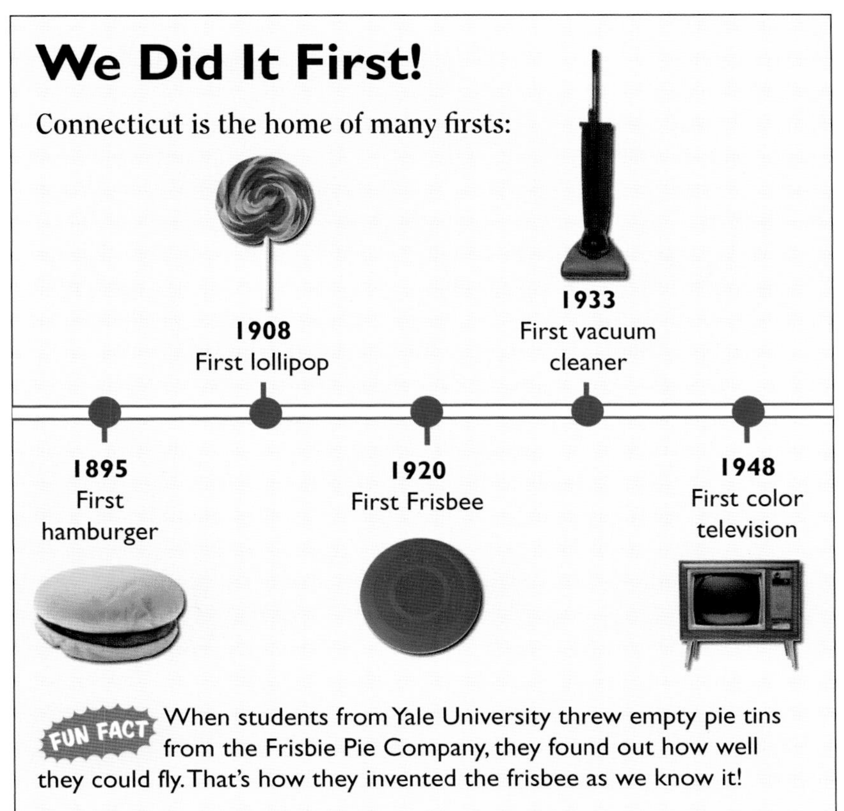

Prehistoric Tracks

At Dinosaur State Park there are tracks in the ground that have been there for a very long time. What animal made the tracks near Rocky Hill, Connecticut? Was it a wild turkey? Could it have been a mountain lion? No, it was a dinosaur! The three-toed fossil tracks were made more than 200 million years ago. They are 10 to 16 inches in length. Paleontologists, scientists who study fossils, think this dinosaur was similar to *Dilophosaurus*.

DID YOU KNOW?

In 1639, Connecticut wrote the first constitution (a set of laws) when it was still a colony. That is why it is called the Constitution State.

The Majestic Charter Oak Tree

In the 1600s, the British tried to control the colonies by taking their constitutions. The early Connecticut leaders did not give theirs up. Instead, they hid it in a huge oak tree. This majestic tree, called Charter Oak, came to stand for a strong spirit and love of freedom. It fell down during a great storm in 1856. Today, there is a memorial where the tree stood. The charter (constitution) was put in a frame made from the tree's wood.

Maine

About 1.3 million people live in Maine. Some are farmers who grow blueberries and potatoes. More blueberries are grown in Maine than in any other state. Other Maine residents work in factories making paper or wood products. Much of the paper used in schools and offices is made here. Maine also makes more toothpicks than any other state. One of the most important industries in Maine is fishing. Fishers catch lobster and lots of other seafood. This seafood is enjoyed throughout the country!

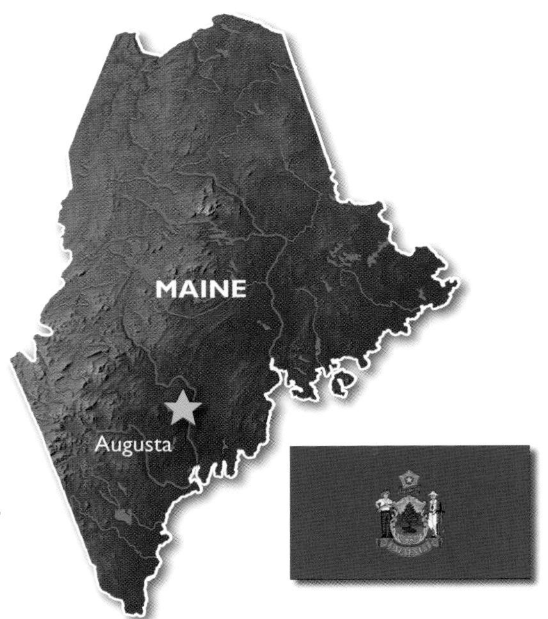

STATE FACTS

Statehood: March 15, 1820—23rd state

Capital: Augusta

Nickname: The Pine Tree State

Motto: I Lead

State Bird: Chickadee

State Flower: White pine cone

First Sunshine!

Where does sunlight first touch the United States? The answer is Maine. This is because Maine is farther east than any other state. The eastern coastline of Maine sits next to the Atlantic Ocean. Rocky beaches line the coast, and there are about 2,000 islands scattered near Maine. Inland, there are colorful forests and rugged mountains. The highest peak in Maine is Mount Katahdin. It is almost a mile high!

Shining Points of Light

A lighthouse has a very important duty. It shines a beam of light out to sea to warn ships of dangerous rocks along the coast. It also helps to guide ships to shore. The coast of Maine has about 60 lighthouses.

FUN FACT The oldest lighthouse is the Portland Head Light, built between 1787 and 1790. It is still working today.

Strong Women from Maine

Margaret Chase Smith

Politician

In 1964, Margaret Chase Smith was nominated, which means selected, to run for president of the United States.

Joan Benoit Samuelson

Athlete

In 1984, Joan Benoit Samuelson won a gold medal in the marathon (26.2 miles) at the Olympics. This was the first time that the marathon was an official event for women athletes.

Samantha Smith

Youngest Ambassador for Peace

In 1983, Samantha Smith went to the Soviet Union to talk to their leader, Yuri Andropov. Their friendship began with a letter she wrote to him about her worries of war. Samantha was ten years old at that time!

The Patient State

During the Revolutionary War, Maine soldiers fought in the Continental Army (the army of the United States). They fought on land and even in sea battles in the waters near the Maine coast. But Maine did not become a state until the year 1820—nearly 44 years after the Declaration of Independence was signed and America had become a country! Do you know why it took so long? It took so long because Maine belonged to Massachusetts. It was known as the District of Maine. Maine finally became an independent state on March 15, 1820. It was the 23rd state.

DID YOU KNOW?

Maine is famous for its wonderful lobster. Fishers must band the claws of lobsters so they can't pinch.

Massachusetts

In 1620, Pilgrims settled the first colony in Massachusetts. Since then, Massachusetts has had a long history of changing the New World. The Revolutionary War against Great Britain began here in 1775. Paul Revere, a messenger in the army, warned the people of the colony that the British were coming. This helped them win the war. Today, more than six million people live in Massachusetts. Some live in the beautiful Berkshire Mountains in the western part of the state. Others live in cities and towns along the central and eastern areas and in the quiet villages on Cape Cod.

Houses on Cape Cod

STATE FACTS

Statehood: February 6, 1788—6th state

Capital: Boston

Nickname: The Bay State

Motto: By the sword we seek peace, but peace only under liberty

State Bird: Black-capped chickadee

State Flower: Mayflower

State Dog: Boston terrier

State Cat: Tabby cat

Massachusetts History = American History

Massachusetts history is an important part of United States history.

Massachusetts was the birthplace of Thanksgiving.

1620 Pilgrims came to the new world on the *Mayflower.* They were seeking religious freedom. They started Plymouth Colony.

1630 The Puritans were another group of people also seeking religious freedom. They formed the Massachusetts Bay Colony near present-day Boston.

1773 Colonists dumped tea in the Boston Harbor. They did not want to be taxed by the King of England.

1775 The Revolutionary War of Independence began in Massachusetts. The first shots were fired in Lexington.

Massachusetts continues to play a large role in the United States. Factory workers make computers, electrical equipment, and scientific instruments.

Bay State Stars

These famous people were born in Massachusetts:

Susan B. Anthony
fought for women's rights

Clara Barton
founder of the American Red Cross

Emily Dickinson
poet

Benjamin Franklin
inventor, publisher, statesman

Theodor Geisel
author known as Dr. Seuss

W. E. B. Du Bois
fought against racism and for civil rights

DID YOU KNOW?

Legend has it that Plymouth Rock in Massachusetts is where the Pilgrims first set down in the New World.

The First to Teach

Harvard University

In 1647, Massachusetts was the first colony to pass a law to make sure every area had schools to teach students. This was the beginning of our country's education system. The oldest high school and oldest college of our nation are in Massachusetts. Today, there are 121 schools for higher learning in this state. Two schools, Harvard University and Massachusetts Institute of Technology, always rank among the best schools in the world.

Lake What...?

A lake near Webster, Massachusetts, has a name that is 45 letters long! It is called Lake Chargoggagoggmanchauggagoggchaubunagungamaugg. The name comes from an Algonquian Indian language spoken by the Nipmuc people. It is the longest name of a place in the United States. (By the way, there is another version of the name that is 49 letters long!)

Hurray for Hoops!

The winters in Springfield, Massachusetts, are cold and snowy. In 1891, James Naismith wanted to create a team sport that people could play indoors. He nailed two peach baskets on opposite sides of the gym. Then he gave players a large ball and 13 rules. Do you know what sport he had invented? You are right! He invented basketball.

You can visit the Naismith Memorial Basketball Hall of Fame. It is located in Springfield, Massachusetts.

New Hampshire

New Hampshire's nickname is the Granite State because its mountains are made of granite rock. The state is also known for its water. It has about 40 rivers. It has about 1,300 lakes and ponds. New Hampshire's eastern border touches the Atlantic Ocean. Its coastline is 18 miles long. Manchester is New Hampshire's largest city and is located on the banks of the Merrimack River.

STATE FACTS

Statehood: June 21, 1788—9th state

Capital: Concord

Nickname: The Granite State

Motto: Live Free or Die

State Bird: Purple finch

State Flower: Purple lilac

State Dog: Chinook

State Butterfly: Karner blue

World of White

People of New Hampshire see white. The White Mountains cover much of the state. The mountains are named after the white granite rock they are made from. White birch trees grow in New Hampshire's forests. Early settlers and Native Americans used the white bark to make roofs, paper, and canoes. New Hampshire's animals also have "white" in their names. The white-tailed deer live in the woods. The white perch live in the lakes. Even the weather is white. In the winter, New Hampshire gets 60 to 100 inches of snow!

We're First!

Every four years, the people of the United States elect a president. Before any election, the states hold primary elections. In these *primaries,* people choose who will get to run for president. New Hampshire is always the first state to hold these primary elections. It has been this way since 1920.

FUN FACT Which New Hampshire residents get to vote first? By law, voters in towns with less than 100 people can vote right after midnight.

Colorful State Symbols

People in New Hampshire love color. The state bird is the purple finch. The state butterfly is the Karner blue. And guess what? The state amphibian is the red-spotted newt. Even the state insect of New Hampshire is colorful. It is red with two black spots. Do you know what it is? It's the ladybug!

Old Man Falls Off Mountain

Do you see the face on this mountain? It is made by five rock ledges. The Old Man of the Mountain was 40 feet tall from his forehead to his chin. In 2003, the face collapsed. But it is not gone forever. You can still see the face on New Hampshire's state quarter.

Faithful Factories

The land in New Hampshire is rocky and hard to farm, so many people work in factories. They make machinery, electrical equipment, and plastic and rubber products. The Globe Manufacturing Company in Pittsfield, New Hampshire, started out as a harness maker in 1887. Today, they make a very important product: firefighting suits!

DID YOU KNOW?

The first free public library in the United States opened in Peterborough, New Hampshire, in 1833.

Polar Caves

About 50,000 years ago, a huge glacier (large slow-moving ice) came down over the White Mountains of New Hampshire. The ice was so big that it moved land and rocks along its path. When the weather warmed up again, the glacier melted some and moved back north. It left behind many caves and passageways in the mountains. Today, you can visit Polar Caves Park and explore all these amazing caves!

Rhode Island

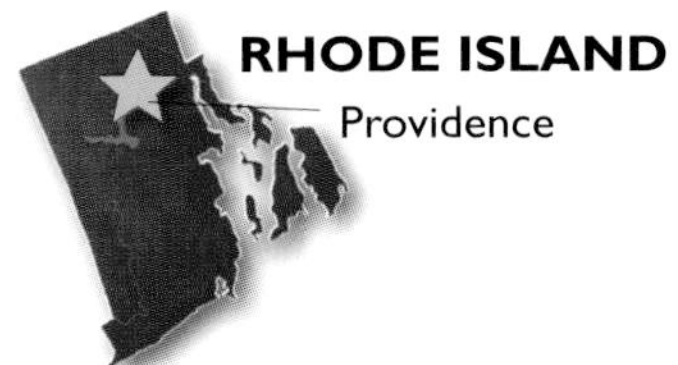

Rhode Island is the smallest state in the country. It is 48 miles long and only 37 miles wide. It is so small that you could drive across it in less than an hour. Though it is called Rhode Island, it is not really an island. But it does have more than 35 islands along its southern coast. If you could stretch out all of Rhode Island's wiggly shores, its coastline would be 400 miles long!

Marble House in Newport

Kicked Out!

Roger Williams founded Rhode Island. In the 1600s, he was part of the Massachusetts Bay Colony. But his ideas about religion were different from the rest of the Puritans, so they kicked him out of the colony. Williams moved south and bought land from the Narragansett Indians. He began a settlement in what is now Rhode Island. It was a safe place for people to worship freely. Today, you can see a statue on top of the capitol in Providence, Rhode Island. It is called the *Independent Man*. The statue is the symbol of Roger Williams' independent and free spirit.

STATE FACTS

Statehood: May 29, 1790—13th state
Capital: Providence
Nickname: The Ocean State
Motto: Hope
State Bird: Rhode Island Red chicken
State Flower: Violet
State Shell: Quahog

Living Sculptures

Can sculptures be alive? Yes! You can see them at the Green Animals Topiary Garden. Since 1872, the thick shrubs have been clipped and shaped to look like animals. The tallest animal is the giraffe. You will also see an elephant, a camel, and a unicorn. There are 21 animals in the garden. It is in Portsmouth, Rhode Island.

Tasty State Symbols

Rhode Island has a state bird that is different from any other state bird. Instead of a bird that can fly, the state symbol for Rhode Island is the Red chicken. It is a breed of chicken that was developed in the 1850s. Red chickens have better meat and eggs than other chickens in the area. These chickens from Rhode Island are sold to all the other states.

Rhode Islanders also enjoy eating the meat of their state shell. It is a hard-shell clam called the "quahog" that lives in Rhode Island's coastal waters. People remove the meat from the shells of these clams and make a soup called clam chowder.

DID YOU KNOW?

Rhode Island was the first colony to declare independence and the last to sign the Constitution of the United States.

Gone Fishin'

Rhode Island used to be full of factories. Now it attracts tourists from across the country. Fishers love to go to Rhode Island. People who fish near the shore catch mackerel, flounder, and bass. People who fish offshore might reel in a tuna, a marlin, a swordfish, or a shark!

Flying Horses?

The oldest operating carousel in the United States is in Watch Park, Rhode Island. It is called the Flying Horses Carousel. There is a good reason for the name. The horses are not attached to the wooden platform. Instead, the horses hang from chains. When the carousel starts spinning, the horses swing to the outside!

FUN FACT Riders can grab metal rings as the carousel goes around. The one with the brass ring at the end of the ride gets to stay on for another free ride.

Vermont

Vermont has a name that describes itself. *Ver* is from a French word that means "green." *Mont* is a French word that means "mountain." So Vermont means green mountain! The Green Mountain range covers much of Vermont. Thousands of years ago, native people hunted in this area for caribou and mastodons. Vermont no longer has caribou or prehistoric mammals. But the state is still full of wilderness and beauty.

The Rural Life

Many people in Vermont live in small towns or on farms. This rural life is the way many make a living. Vermont has more dairies than any other state in New England. Cows and goats make milk for dairy products. Vermont is also known for tourism. People from across the country visit Vermont in the fall to see the brilliant leaves of the trees.

FUN FACT If you've ever eaten a scoop of Ben & Jerry's ice cream, it may have come from the milk of a Vermont cow.

Strange Creatures

In 1849, railroad workers digging in the ground near Burlington, Vermont, made a huge discovery. They found the fossil of a whale that was about 11,500 years old! The reason the bones of a whale were found on land and not at sea is because long ago the ocean covered the land in Vermont. The whale fossil was nicknamed Charlotte.

Vermont has another sea creature, but this one is still alive today. It is a 20-foot sea serpent that lives in Lake Champlain. This creature has a nickname too: Champ.

Lighthouse on Lake Champlain

Maple Sweetness

Vermont makes more maple syrup than any other state. Maple syrup is made from the sap of the sugar maple tree.

Here's the old-fashioned way to get sap out of a tree:

1. Drill a few holes into the tree.
2. Place faucets in the holes.
3. Hang a bucket underneath the faucet.
4. Wait for the sap to drip out of the tree.

It takes about 40 gallons of sap to make one gallon of pure maple syrup. No wonder it tastes so good!

STATE FACTS

Statehood: March 4, 1791—14th state

Capital: Montpelier

Nickname: The Green Mountain State

Motto: Vermont, Freedom and Unity

State Bird: Hermit thrush

State Flower: Red clover

Free to Be Independent

The people in Vermont have always liked their independence. In 1777, they decided *not* to join the other 13 colonies when they formed the United States. Vermont formed its own country instead. They had their own coins and postal service. They also wrote their own constitution, which is a set of laws. In 1791, Vermont decided to join the United States. They were the 14th state and the first one to enter the Union after the original 13 colonies.

DID YOU KNOW?

Vermont is home to 107 historic covered bridges.

Mid-Atlantic

Skyscrapers, factories, banks, and museums—the Mid-Atlantic region is full of people, buildings, and action. Some of the nation's major cities are in this area, including New York, Philadelphia, and Baltimore. This region also has major waterways. Ships move goods along the Chesapeake Bay, the Hudson River, and the Delaware River. The Mid-Atlantic region stretches to the west and has large areas of farmland, forest, hills, and mountains.

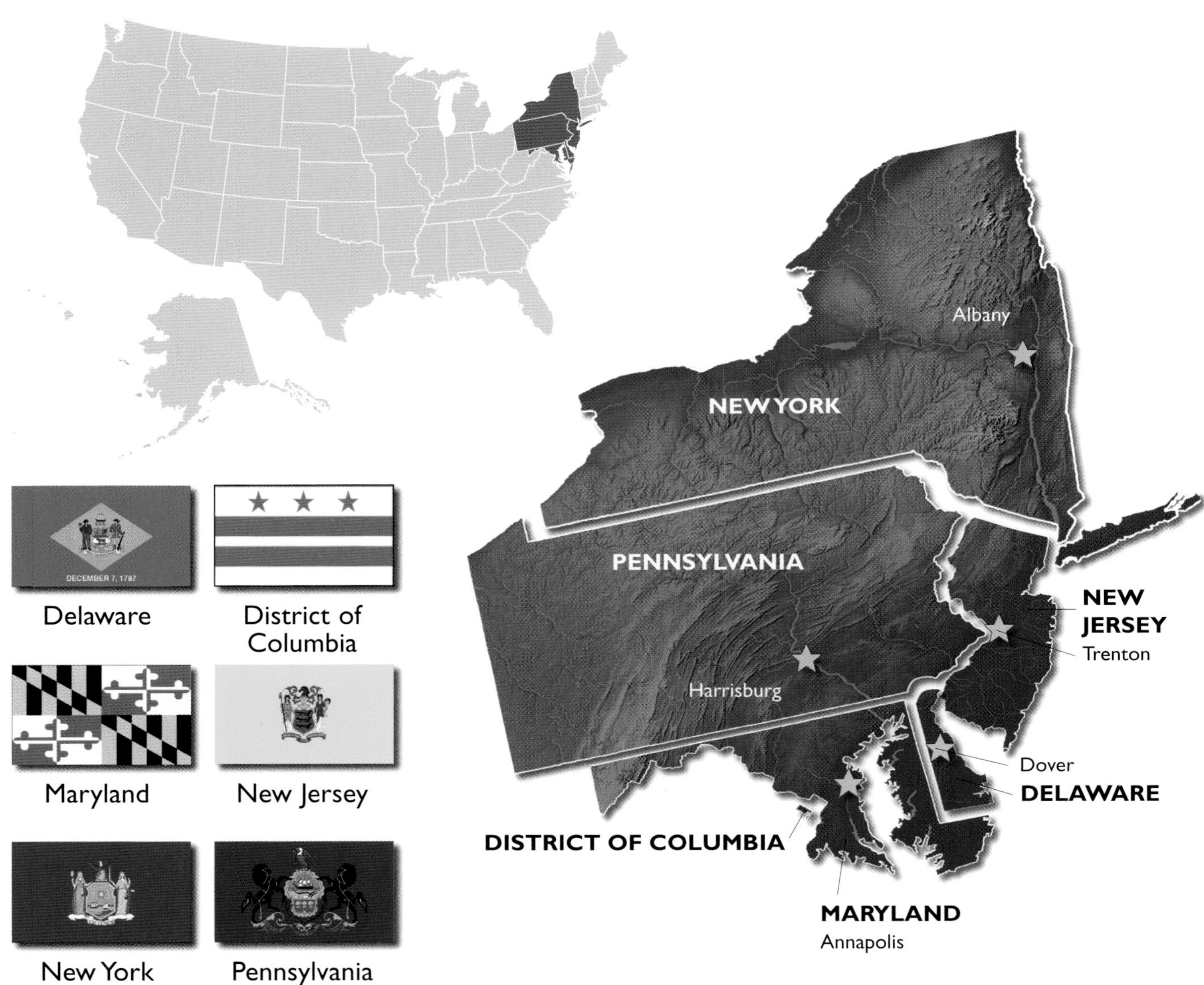

Together From the Start

The states of the Mid-Atlantic were among the original 13 colonies. They have been together since the very start of our nation. Delaware, Pennsylvania, and New Jersey were the first three colonies to become states. The Mid-Atlantic states still have many things in common today. Each state has large factories that produces goods. All but one state has major ports where ships can dock. The Mid-Atlantic region has rural areas full of farms that grow poultry and fruit, and make dairy products. Farms in the northern part of the region grow apples and grapes. In the south and along the coast, the weather is great for growing peaches!

An Ocean Away?

Look at the map of the Mid-Atlantic region. Notice that every state except one touches the Atlantic Ocean. Which state is not touching the Atlantic Ocean? Pennsylvania. This bothered the people of Pennsylvania when it was still a colony. At one time, Pennsylvania took control of Delaware so it could have a path to the ocean. It was important for a state to be near the ocean and waterways since the fastest way to move goods back then was by ship. Today, goods are also moved by airplanes, trucks, and trains.

Sharing Freedom

The Statue of Liberty looks across New York Harbor, but the island that she stands upon is also close to New Jersey! The Statue of Liberty doesn't belong to a state or a specific region. She was a gift to the United States from France. She is a symbol of freedom, welcoming people to America with a poem. Here's part of that poem:

The New Colossus

Give me your tired, your poor,
Your huddled masses yearning
to breathe free,
The wretched refuse of your
teeming shore.
Send these, the homeless,
tempest-tossed to me,
I lift my lamp beside the
golden door!
—Emma Lazarus

The New York Giants play the New York Jets.

Are You Ready for Some Football?

Many professional sports teams have homes in the Mid-Atlantic region. If you are a football fan, you are lucky because you can watch seven different football teams! All of the teams belong to the National Football League (NFL).

Baltimore Ravens
New York Jets
Buffalo Bills
Philadelphia Eagles
New York Giants
Pittsburgh Steelers
Washington Redskins

Delaware

Delaware's nickname is the First State. This nickname is a good one. On December 7, 1787, Delaware became the first state to ratify, which means approve, the United States Constitution. Delaware also has the nickname "Small Wonder." Even though it is the second smallest state, it is an interesting place to visit.

STATE FACTS

Statehood: December 7, 1787—1st state

Capital: Dover

Nickname: The First State

Motto: Liberty and Independence

State Bird: Blue hen

State Flower: Peach blossom

State Fish: Weakfish

Riding Toward Independence

In 1776, leaders from the 13 colonies met in Philadelphia on July 2. They were going to vote if they should break free from British rule. Caeser Rodney was the leader from Delaware. But on July 1, he was still in Delaware. He was busy fighting those who wanted to stay with Britain. He rode 80 miles on horseback through a stormy night. He reached Philadelphia just in time the next day. With the help of his vote, every colony voted to be free of Great Britain.

Where Did the Birds Fly?

Every spring, thousands of Red Knots fly from the southern tip of South America to Delaware Bay. When they arrive, they are nearly starved. For the next two weeks, they eat the tiny eggs of the horseshoe crabs. Each bird eats about 25,000 eggs a day. But there is a problem. For the last few years, the number of Red Knots has become smaller. This is because the number of horseshoe crabs has also dropped, and the Red Knots need to feed on them to survive. People in Delaware are worried that the Red Knots may die out and never return.

Holy Trinity Old Swedes Church in Wilmington

First in Chemicals

The Swedes were the first Europeans to settle in Delaware. They built log cabins. These may have been the first log cabins in the United States. Today, Delaware has a large number of factories that produce chemicals and chemical products. People gave a nickname to the city of Wilmington, where most of these factories are built. They call this city the "Chemical Capital of the World." One company in Wilmington, Delaware, is the world leader in making chemicals. That company is DuPont.

Mark Your Calendar

What do people in Delaware do for fun? Check your calendars!

March: Chocolate Festival in Rehoboth Beach

September: Jazz Funeral at Bethany Beach to mourn the end of summer

November: Return Day in Georgetown. The day after an election, a town crier reads the election results. The winner and loser ride in the parade together.

Return Day in Georgetown

DID YOU KNOW?

Delaware was named after Lord de la Warr, the first governor of Virginia.

Fighting Blue Hens

During the Revolutionary War, soldiers from Delaware carried fighting roosters into battle. The fiercest roosters were the sons of a Blue Hen. The soldiers called themselves "Blue Hen's Chickens." As the soldiers would go into battle, they would chant: "We're sons of the Blue Hen, and we're game to the end!"

The Blue Hen is the mascot for the University of Delaware sports teams.

District of Columbia

DISTRICT OF COLUMBIA

The city of Washington is the capital of the United States. But Washington is not one of the 50 states! Instead, it is in an area called the District of Columbia (D.C.). Hundreds of years ago, this land was full of wildlife. Deer, wild turkeys, and frogs lived in the woods and the wetlands. Today, this area is full of people and beautiful buildings. It is also the home of the president of the United States.

United States Capitol, Washington, D.C.

A Rough Start

In 1800, President John Adams moved into the White House. But it was not called the White House then. Instead, people called it the President's House. When James Madison was president, something horrible happened. In 1814, the British invaded the city. They burned down the President's House! After that, President Madison lived in the Octagon House.

Three years later, President James Monroe moved into the rebuilt President's House. People nicknamed it the "White House" because it was all white on the outside. In 1901, President Theodore Roosevelt made the nickname official, and since then everyone has called it the White House.

The White House, home to the president, is the most visited home in the United States.

A Riddle of Friendship

We came to Washington, D.C., from Japan in 1912. There were 3,000 of us. In 1965, Japan sent more of us to Washington. Our ancestor is 1,500 years old. Do you know who we are? We are cherry trees!

Japan gave Washington, D.C., the cherry trees as a symbol of friendship. Washington, D.C., celebrates the blooming of the cherry trees with a two-week festival every spring.

Landmarks in Our Nation's Capital

Washington, D.C., is full of famous landmarks. Many of them are historic monuments or memorials built as a way to honor our nation's past. A few of the most famous and important are:

Washington Monument

Built in honor of our first president, George Washington. It took 36 years to build, from 1848 to 1884. This type of monument is an obelisk.

Jefferson Memorial

Built in honor of a founding father and third president, Thomas Jefferson. It was completed in 1943. The Jefferson Memorial is a neoclassical building.

Lincoln Memorial

Built in honor of our 16th president, Abraham Lincoln. It was completed in 1922. This is a memorial in the style of a temple.

DID YOU KNOW?

The address of the White House is 1600 Pennsylvania Avenue, Washington, D.C.

DISTRICT FACTS

Motto: Justice for All

Bird: Wood thrush

Flower: American beauty rose

Tree: Scarlet oak

D.C. Information

The District of Columbia

Location:

- Bordered on three sides by Maryland
- Bordered on one side by Virginia
- Located on the north bank of the Potomac River
- City of Washington covers the full area of the District of Columbia

History:

- City designed by Frenchman Pierre-Charles L'Enfant
- City planned out by Andrew Ellicott and Benjamin Banneker

People:

- About 600,000 people live in Washington, D.C.
- People who live in this city are the only ones in the United States who do not elect politicians to Congress because Washington, D.C., is not a state.

Maryland

The state of Maryland has an amazing shape. The eastern part of Maryland wraps itself around the water of the Chesapeake Bay. The western part of Maryland is not wide at all, but it reaches far into the Appalachian Mountains. More than five million people live in Maryland. Many people work in factories. Other people work for the federal government in offices and laboratories. In rural areas, people grow and sell nursery products, such as flowers, shrubs, and fruit trees.

STATE FACTS

Statehood: April 28, 1788—7th state
Capital: Annapolis
Nickname: The Old Line State
Motto: Strong Deeds, Gentle Words
State Bird: Baltimore oriole
State Flower: Black-eyed Susan
State Reptile: Diamondback terrapin
State Crustacean: Maryland blue crab

DID YOU KNOW?

Western Maryland is very narrow. One part of the state is less than two miles wide!

Chesapeake Bay Traffic

Ships have traveled the Chesapeake Bay for almost 400 years. Settlers from England came to Maryland in 1634. They sailed up the Chesapeake Bay in two small ships: the *Ark* and the *Dove*. They settled on tiny St. Clements Island on the western shore. Today, barges travel up the Chesapeake Bay. They move goods from Baltimore and other cities along the bay. Chesapeake Bay is also the home of Maryland's state boat, the skipjack. About 100 years ago, fishers used this sailboat when they fished oysters from the bottom of the bay. Only a few of these boats remain today.

Baltimore Harbor

Where Salt and Fresh Water Meet

Chesapeake Bay has salt water *and* fresh water. The salt water enters from the Atlantic Ocean. Fresh water enters from the Susquehanna, Potomac, and James Rivers that flow into the bay. When a body of water contains fresh water and salt water, it is called an *estuary*. Chesapeake Bay is the biggest estuary in the United States. The Chesapeake Bay area has more than 3,600 types of plant and animal life. Look at the photos of a few of these amazing animals.

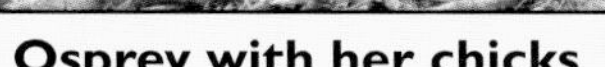

Osprey with her chicks

Maryland blue crabs

Diamondback terrapin (turtle)

Chesapeake Bay got its name from the Algonquin Indian word *Chesepioc*, which means "village by a big river."

Maryland Heroes

Harriet Tubman

Harriet Tubman was born into slavery in Dorchester County, Maryland. When she was 29 years old, she escaped. She went back to the south 19 times. She helped more than 300 slaves escape to freedom through the Underground Railroad.

Frederick Douglass

Frederick Douglass was born in Easton, Maryland, on the eastern shore of Maryland. He was also a slave. He escaped to Massachusetts when he was 20 by working at a shipyard. Later, he became an abolitionist (someone who fights for the freedom of slaves). He traveled the country making speeches against the evils of slavery.

The Star-Spangled Banner

Our national anthem was written during the War of 1812. Some people call this the Second Revolutionary War. It was a scary time. British soldiers were burning buildings throughout Maryland and Washington. A man named Francis Scott Key watched as the British attacked Fort McHenry near Baltimore. In the morning, he noticed that the United States flag was still there! He was so inspired that he wrote a poem called "The Star-Spangled Banner." It became our national anthem.

Oh, say can you see, by the dawn's early light,
What so proudly we hail'd at the twilight's last gleaming?
Whose broad stripes and bright stars, thro' the perilous fight,
O'er the ramparts we watch'd, were so gallantly streaming?
And the rockets' red glare, the bombs bursting in air,
Gave proof thro' the night that our flag was still there.
O say, does that star-spangled banner yet wave
O'er the land of the free and the home of the brave?

New Jersey

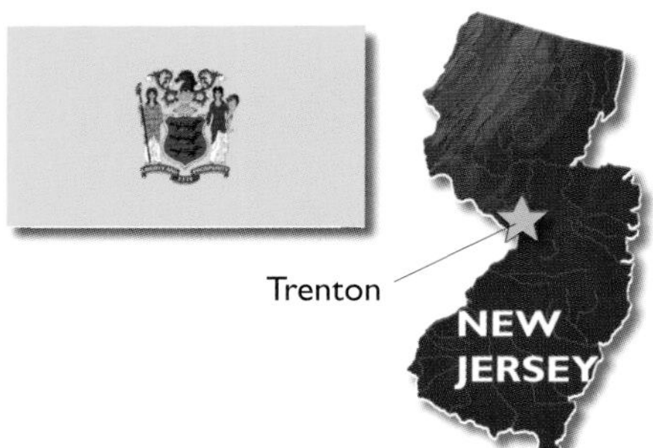

Hundreds of years ago, the Lenape Indians hunted, fished, and farmed in what is now New Jersey. In the 1600s, settlers from the Netherlands, Sweden, and England came to live on this land. New Jersey is a busy place today. More than eight million people live in this small state. About 1,100 people live in every square mile. That means that no other state packs as many people into so little space.

STATE FACTS

Statehood: Dec. 18, 1787—3rd state
Capital: Trenton
Nickname: The Garden State
Motto: Liberty and Prosperity
State Flower: Violet
State Bird: Eastern goldfinch
State Dinosaur: *Hadrosaurus foulkii*

It Happened in New Jersey

It was Christmas night in 1776. The air was cold. The river was almost frozen. But George Washington and his soldiers paddled their boat across the Delaware River. The next morning they surprised the enemy at Trenton and won the battle. This was an important victory during the Revolutionary War. A picture honoring Washington and his men is on the New Jersey state quarter.

DID YOU KNOW?

President Grover Cleveland was born in New Jersey. He served as the 22nd and 24th president of the United States.

Beach in Cape May

Work and Play

Most people in New Jersey live in large towns and cities. Some of them travel to New York City and Philadelphia to work. Others work in factories in New Jersey. Many people in these factories make chemicals, printed materials, and food products. New Jersey also has good places for people to vacation. People can ski in the north or relax on the beaches of Cape May in the south. People like to go to Atlantic City on the eastern shore. It has fancy hotels, a boardwalk, and amusement parks.

A State of Gardens

New Jersey is nicknamed the Garden State for good reason. It is home to almost 10,000 farms covering only a small area of land. New Jersey farms grow blueberries, cranberries, bell peppers, and peaches. The state is also famous for having many horses. There are more horses per square mile in New Jersey than any other state.

Though known as the Garden State, New Jersey has the most crowded system of highways and railroads in the country.

A Bright Idea

Thomas Edison is a famous American inventor. He invented many things, such as the motion picture camera and the electric lightbulb. He opened the first research lab in Menlo Park, New Jersey, in 1876.

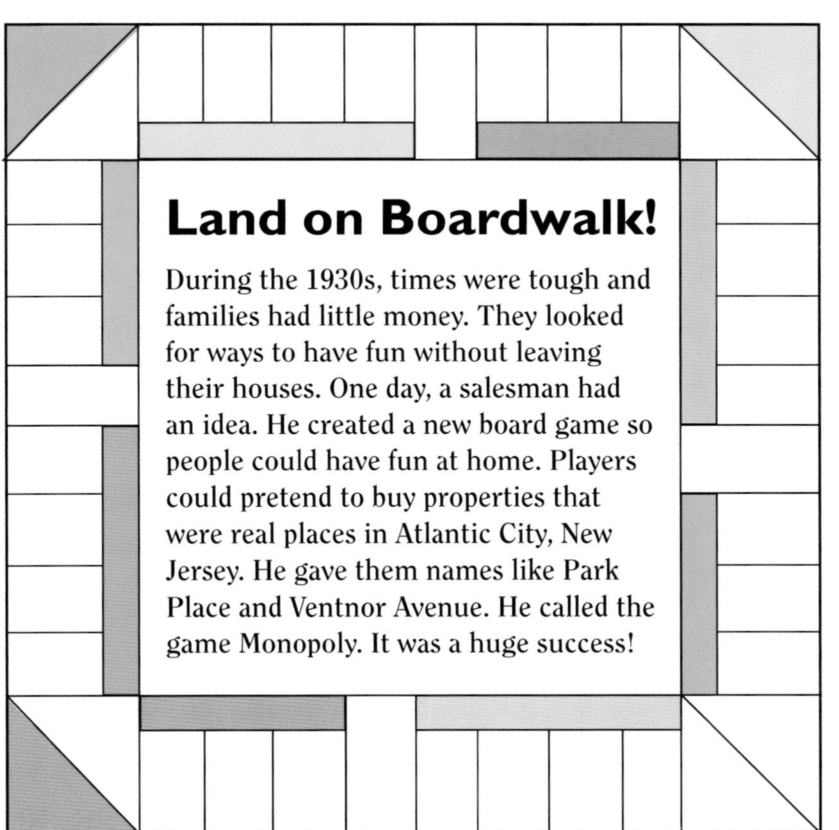

Land on Boardwalk!

During the 1930s, times were tough and families had little money. They looked for ways to have fun without leaving their houses. One day, a salesman had an idea. He created a new board game so people could have fun at home. Players could pretend to buy properties that were real places in Atlantic City, New Jersey. He gave them names like Park Place and Ventnor Avenue. He called the game Monopoly. It was a huge success!

Buried Treasure

William Kidd was a pirate. In the 1690s, he buried treasure on the shore of New Jersey. It is said that Kidd's treasure is all gold! People today are still searching for his treasure.

William Parker Foulke was visiting New Jersey in 1858. What did he find in Haddonfield? Dinosaur bones! You can still see the narrow valley where he found the nearly complete dinosaur skeleton.

New York

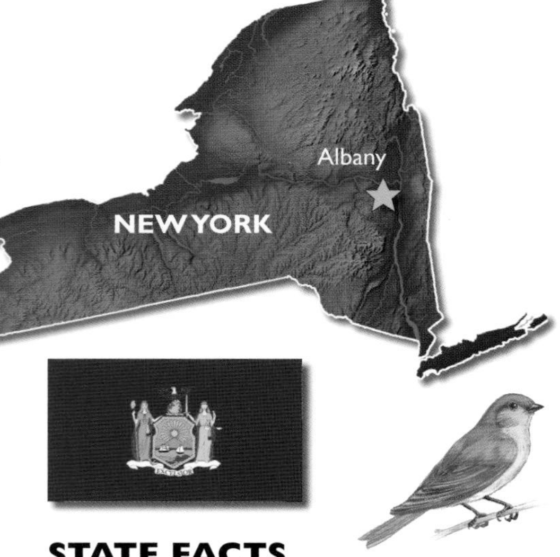

Forests once covered most of the state of New York. An explorer, Henry Hudson, took over the land for the Dutch in 1609. This area turned out to be popular for many new settlers. The British took the colony from the Dutch in 1664. Since then, New York has grown to become a giant of business. Today, it makes more goods and provides more services than many countries do, even though it is just a state!

STATE FACTS

Statehood: July 26, 1788—11th state
Capital: Albany
Nickname: The Empire State
Motto: Excelsior (Ever Upward)
State Bird: Bluebird
State Flower: Rose
State Gem: Garnet
State Animal: Beaver

The Answer Is Erie

New Yorkers had a problem. How could they move goods across the state? There wasn't a good road between Albany and Buffalo. They solved their problem by digging the Erie Canal. They began work on the canal in 1817. By 1825, it was finished and full of water. Before long, mules were pulling barges across the state. The Erie Canal also allowed people to move goods from faraway New York City to the Great Lakes.

DID YOU KNOW?

The *New York Post*, first printed in 1803 by Alexander Hamilton, is the oldest running newspaper in the United States.

Niagara Falls

Niagara Falls is on the Niagara River between Lake Ontario and Lake Erie. More than 12 million people visit Niagara Falls each year. Niagara Falls includes the American Falls and Horseshoe Falls. The American Falls has a 70- to 100-foot drop. The water is moved through tunnels and pipes to a hydroelectric station. Turbines (spinning motors) use the power of the water to turn and make electricity for part of New York.

A Very Short History of New York City

New York City is built on Manhattan Island. In 1626, the Dutch bought this land from the Lenape Indians and called it "New Amsterdam." But the Dutch did not keep it. In 1664, the British took over the island and named it "New York." But the British could not hold on to New York either. After the Revolutionary War, the Americans took control. From 1785 to 1790, New York City was the capital of the United States. Today, New York City is home to more than eight million Americans. It leads the nation in fashion, art, banking, and entertainment.

Now That's a Park!

The Adirondack Park is a six-million-acre piece of land that is protected by the state of New York. It is about the size of Vermont! More than 400 different kinds of animals live in the rugged Adirondack mountains. These include coyotes, foxes, wolves, bobcats, mountain lions, black bears, and timber rattlesnakes. Many types of birds also live in the Adirondack Park. You can see bald eagles, turkey buzzards, and falcons in this park.

Chautauqua Camp?

In 1874, people from Chautauqua, New York, started an adult learning movement that still goes on today. This movement took the name of the town. Chautauqua is a way to bring together many people to teach and learn about different ideas, views, and arts. They bring speakers, teachers, musicians, preachers, and specialists to their small town. They gather during the pleasant summer months. Their gatherings are like summer camps, where learning, playing, worshiping, and entertaining all take place. Many other small towns today also hold such events, but it all started in Chautauqua.

Miracle on Ice

Lake Placid, New York, was the home of the 1932 and 1980 Winter Olympics. In the 1980 Olympics, the United States hockey team beat the Soviet Union by a score of 4–3. No one thought the United States would win. Their team was made of young college students. The Soviet team was made of paid professional players. Today, athletes still compete in winter sports at Lake Placid. Many tourists also visit Lake Placid each year.

FUN FACT Visitors to Lake Placid can take bobsled rides down the Olympic track!

New York Years

1609	Henry Hudson sails up the Hudson River, which is named after him. He claims the land for the Dutch.
1626	The Dutch buy Manhattan Island from the American Indians.
1664	The British take control. They call the settlement New York.
1776	New York (and other colonies) declare independence from Great Britain.
1788	New York becomes the 11th state.
1883	The Brooklyn Bridge opens.
1952	United Nations headquarters opens in New York City.
2001	World Trade Center is attacked by terrorists.

Statues at Women's Rights National Historical Par

No Fair!

Years ago, women were not allowed to vote. They could not own property or go to most colleges. Elizabeth Cady Stanton and four other women decided to change that. On July 19–20, 1848, they held the First Woman's Rights Convention in Seneca Falls, New York. One hundred women and men promised to work for equal rights for women. In 1920, women won the right to vote and to have the same rights as men.

One City—Five Parts

New York City has five parts. These are called boroughs (pronounced *bur-rows*). They are Manhattan, the Bronx, Brooklyn, Staten Island, and Queens. The Empire State Building and Grand Central Station are in Manhattan. Central Park, Wall Street, and Times Square are also found here. Manhattan is the busiest part of New York City.

A Place for All Nations

The United Nations headquarters is in New York City. People from 192 different countries (or *nations*) meet here. They talk about ways to solve world problems. If you go on a tour of the United Nations headquarters, keep your ears open. Many languages of the world are spoken here.

Baseball Hall of Fame

The National Baseball Hall of Fame is in Cooperstown, New York. This museum is full of baseball history. It has gloves, baseballs, caps, and photographs of famous baseball players. The Hall of Fame honors the very best baseball players. Almost 300 people have been elected to the Hall of Fame.

DID YOU KNOW?

New York was the first state to pass a law to make every car have a license plate.

How Long Is the Island?

New York has an island that stretches into the Atlantic Ocean. It is 118 miles long. (Maybe this is why it's called Long Island!) Kennedy Airport and LaGuardia Airport are on the western part of Long Island. The eastern part of Long Island has many beaches. People have beautiful summer homes on this part of Long Island.

Big Park in a Big City

Central Park is a large park in the middle of Manhattan. It has trees, lakes, and walking trails. It also has baseball fields and 21 playgrounds. There is even a zoo! Central Park is a half mile wide and 2.5 miles long. The park gives people from New York a place to play and relax.

FUN FACT Central Park was the first public park built in America. Started in 1858, it took 15 years and $14 million to build the park.

Pennsylvania

Pennsylvania means "Penn's woods." In 1681, King Charles of England gave the land to William Penn, who set up a colony. Almost a hundred years later, the people of the colonies wanted their own country. In Pennsylvania, in a city called Philadelphia (which means "brotherly love"), the leaders of the new nation came together to declare their freedom from England.

William Penn

STATE FACTS

Statehood: December 12, 1787—2nd state
Capital: Harrisburg
Nickname: The Keystone State
Motto: Virtue, Liberty, and Independence
State Bird: Ruffed grouse
State Flower: Mountain laurel
State Insect: Firefly
State Dog: Great Dane

What's in Pennsylvania?

Pittsburgh and Philadelphia are the largest cities in Pennsylvania. Pittsburgh sits between three rivers in the western part of the state. Philadelphia is in the southeastern part of the state. Between these cities, there are forests, rolling mountains, and miles of farmland. Farmers grow hay, oats, potatoes, peaches, corn, and grapes. They also grow more mushrooms than any other state. Pennsylvania has a treasure deep below the ground. It is called coal. Pennsylvania's coal is an important source of energy for our country.

Battle of Gettysburg

During the 1860s, America fought a civil war to end slavery. One of the most famous battles of the war took place at Gettysburg, Pennsylvania. The Union Army, which was from the North, beat General Robert E. Lee and his Confederate Army of the South. The battle began on July 1, 1863. It took only three days to fight, but it changed the direction of the war. It saved America from splitting into two countries!

Big Events in United States History

Many important events happened in Philadelphia.

1753
Liberty Bell first hung

1776
Declaration of Independence signed

1787
United States Constitution written

1790
Philadelphia becomes capital of the United States

Philadelphia remained the capital of the United States until 1800. After that, Washington, D.C., became the capital.

Furry and Famous

Punxsutawney Phil is a famous groundhog. On February 2 of each year, he predicts the weather. If Phil sees his shadow, there will be six more weeks of winter. If Phil doesn't see his shadow, spring will come soon. People have celebrated Groundhog Day in Punxsutawney since 1887. Of course, the original Phil isn't around anymore.

When each "Punxsutawney Phil" retires, a new groundhog is chosen.

Who Are the Amish?

If you go to southeastern Pennsylvania, you might see horse-drawn wagons. These belong to the Amish. They do not use cars, electricity, telephones, or modern technology. The Amish believe it is important to lead a simple life that values family, community, and peace. Because of this, they choose to separate themselves from the modern world.

DID YOU KNOW?

Fred Rogers was born in Latrobe, Pennsylvania. His television show was called *Mister Rogers' Neighborhood.*

Midwest

The land of the Midwest seems flat, but it has gentle slopes and hills. It is great for farming. The Midwest is the home of the prairie. The Mississippi River, the longest river in the United States, begins as a small brook in northern Minnesota. Then it widens as it flows to the south. The Great Lakes are also in the Midwest. These five lakes make up the largest area of fresh water in the world.

Illinois

Indiana

Iowa

Kansas

Michigan

Minnesota

Missouri

Nebraska

North Dakota

Ohio

South Dakota

Wisconsin

Breadbasket of America

Settlers first came to the Midwest in the 1800s. They knew the land for farming was better here than in the eastern part of the country. Today, there are many farms in the Midwest. The rich soil, warm sunshine, and soaking rains all help grow good crops. Farmers grow corn, wheat, and soybeans. They also raise cattle, hogs, and turkeys. Midwesterners raise food for people all across the United States. No wonder this land is called "America's Breadbasket."

Where to Make Things

Since the 1800s, the Midwest has been a great location for making products. The Great Lakes waterway allows ships to move coal, iron ore, and other raw materials. People who work in factories along the lakes and rivers use the materials to make steel, tools, machines, and cars.

How's the Weather?

In the Midwest, the summers are often hot. Winters are cold with snow. The weather in the Midwest can also be harsh. Strong winds, severe thunderstorms, and tornadoes often go through this area. People from the Midwest know to keep an eye on the sky.

Chicago: City by the Lake

Chicago is the largest city in the Midwest. It is the third largest city in the United States. Because of its size and location, it acts as a hub. It is a connecting point for trucks, trains, and air traffic to the rest of the country. People and goods can go anywhere from Chicago.

Illinois

The state of Illinois is in the middle of the Midwest. It is in the middle of the action! Large companies in Illinois make machines, food products, metal products, and chemicals. Trucks and trains travel in many directions to deliver goods. Even the countryside is busy. Farmers grow corn, soybeans, hay, and wheat. They also raise cattle and hogs.

ILLINOIS

STATE FACTS

Statehood: December 3, 1818—21st state
Capital: Springfield
Nickname: The Prairie State
Motto: State Sovereignty—National Union

State Bird: Cardinal
State Flower: Violet
State Snack Food: Popcorn
State Fish: Bluegill
State Amphibian: Eastern tiger salamander

This farm in Illinois is growing soybeans.

The Prairie State

Illinois is called the Prairie State. Long ago, it was covered with long prairie grass. The Native Americans who first lived on this prairie were called the "Illini" or "Illiniwek." When explorers from France came to this land, they named the land Illinois (il-uh-NOY). Today, the original prairie has nearly disappeared. Over 12 million people live in Illinois. More than half of them live in or near the city of Chicago.

Lincoln Lived Here

One of the most famous people to live in Illinois is Abraham Lincoln. He was born in Kentucky, lived in Indiana, then moved to Illinois when he was 21 years old. At first, he lived in New Salem. He spent most of his life in Springfield, where he raised his family and worked as a lawyer. He lived there until he was elected president in 1860. If you go to Springfield today, you can visit his house and where he is buried.

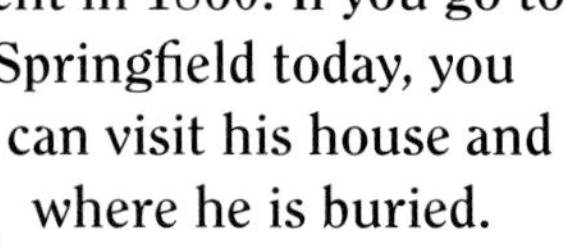

DID YOU KNOW?

President Ronald Reagan was born in Tampico, Illinois.

John Deere Green

John Deere is not just the name of a tractor. It is also the name of a person. John Deere moved to Grand Detour, Illinois, in 1837. He invented the steel plow there. Later, he moved to Moline, Illinois, and made more plows and farm equipment. Today, the John Deere Company is known worldwide for its farm machines and tools. It is still based in Moline, Illinois.

The Great Chicago Fire

In 1871, a great fire burned through most of Chicago. The city's closely built wooden houses fed the fire. It burned for more than 24 hours and left 90,000 people homeless. But after the fire, the people of Chicago did not give up. Talented builders and hard workers rebuilt the city. Chicago is now known for its beautiful buildings and amazing skyline.

Sky-high Tower

The tallest building in the United States is in Chicago, Illinois. It used to be called Sears Tower. Now it has a new name: Willis Tower. It has 110 stories and is 1,451 feet high. People can take an elevator to the 103rd floor. They can look out of the large windows and see the city, lake, and land for many miles around. On a clear day, you can see three other states: Wisconsin, Indiana, and Michigan. You can also step on a see-through glass floor and look 1,353 feet straight down!

FUN FACT The tower was built to withstand storms and high winds. To do this, it can sway six inches to each side.

Indiana

Before Indiana was a state, it was called Indian Territory. It stretched into present-day Illinois and north to Canada. Native Americans lived in the Indian Territory. So did Native Americans who had been pushed out of the eastern part of the United States. Indiana became a state in 1816. Five years earlier, the United States Army had defeated one of the last groups of Native Americans in the area. Today, less than 8,000 Native Americans live in Indiana.

A buck (male deer) lives in a forest in Indiana.

This Indiana farmer is working with two bulls.

Hoosier Life

Indiana is a major factory and farming state. Workers in Indiana make steel, medicine, medical tools, electrical equipment, and chemical products. Farming is also very important in Indiana. Farmers grow corn, soybeans, melons, tomatoes, grapes, and mint. They also fatten cattle and hogs in feedlots. In the southern part of the state, furniture-making is big business. Workers use the wood from walnut trees that still grow on the land to make furniture.

The "Mad" General

Fort Wayne in Indiana was built in 1794 to protect the early settlers from Native American raids. The fort was named after General "Mad" Anthony Wayne. The general earned the nickname "Mad" because of his daring attacks against British soldiers during the Revolutionary War. The army fort was remade in 1816 and still stands today. Visitors can go there to see military demonstrations.

Indiana Dunes

Indiana has a national lakeshore. It is on the shore of Lake Michigan between two steel mills. The highest dune is Mount Baldy. It is 126 feet high. Because it moves four feet each year, it is called a "living dune." Unfortunately, Mount Baldy is starving. The waves of Lake Michigan are slowly washing away its sand.

STATE FACTS

Statehood: December 11, 1816—19th state

Capital: Indianapolis

Nickname: The Hoosier State

Motto: The Crossroads of America

State Bird: Cardinal

State Flower: Peony

State Tree: Tulip Tree

State Stone: Indiana limestone

State Song: "On the Banks of the Wabash, Far Away"

Who's a Hoosier?

Indiana is called the Hoosier State. No one is sure how the state got that nickname, but people who come from Indiana are called Hoosiers. Here are some famous Hoosiers:

Benjamin Harrison
23rd president of the United States

Frank Borman
commander of the *Apollo 8* mission

Michael Jackson
singer, songwriter

Larry Bird
champion basketball player

Florence Henderson
actress

James Dean
actor

Start Your Engines!

Every year, the biggest race in the country takes place in Indiana. It is a famous race called the Indianapolis 500. Racecars have been racing here since 1911. Over time, the racecars have become much faster. Only 33 cars are allowed to race each year. They race for 500 miles. For coming in first, the winner receives a trophy, a wreath, and a glass of milk!

FUN FACT Ray Harroun won the first race at the Indianapolis 500. He drove a yellow car called the Marmon Wasp.

DID YOU KNOW?

The world's first theme park opened in Santa Claus, Indiana, on August 3, 1946. It is called Holiday World.

Iowa

Iowa grows a large share of our nation's food. More soybeans and corn are grown in Iowa than any other state. More hogs are raised here too. Iowa is also among the top states that raise cows for beef. Many people from Iowa work in factories packing meat. Iowa also makes lots of fun foods. Sioux City, Iowa, is the home of Palmer Candy and Jolly Time Popcorn.

STATE FACTS

Statehood: December 28, 1846—29th state
Capital: Des Moines
Nickname: The Hawkeye State
Motto: Our Liberties We Prize and Our Rights We Will Maintain
State Bird: Eastern goldfinch
State Flower: Wild rose
State Song: "Song of Iowa"
State Tree: Northern red oak

More Farms for Iowa?

Iowa does not have just land farms. It has wind farms too. The large areas of open land are great for windmills. A school in Spirit Lake, Iowa, was one of the first schools to use wind energy. It built their windmill and placed it in the school's playground in 1993. Today, Iowa has more than 1,000 windmills, and the number keeps growing.

Here's how windmills work: The blowing wind turns the blades of the windmill. The turning blades spin a turbine (a spinning motor). The spinning of the motor makes electricity. The weather in Iowa is great for wind farms. The turbines need wind that blows at least 14 miles per hour. This isn't a problem. In northwest Iowa, the wind is always blowing.

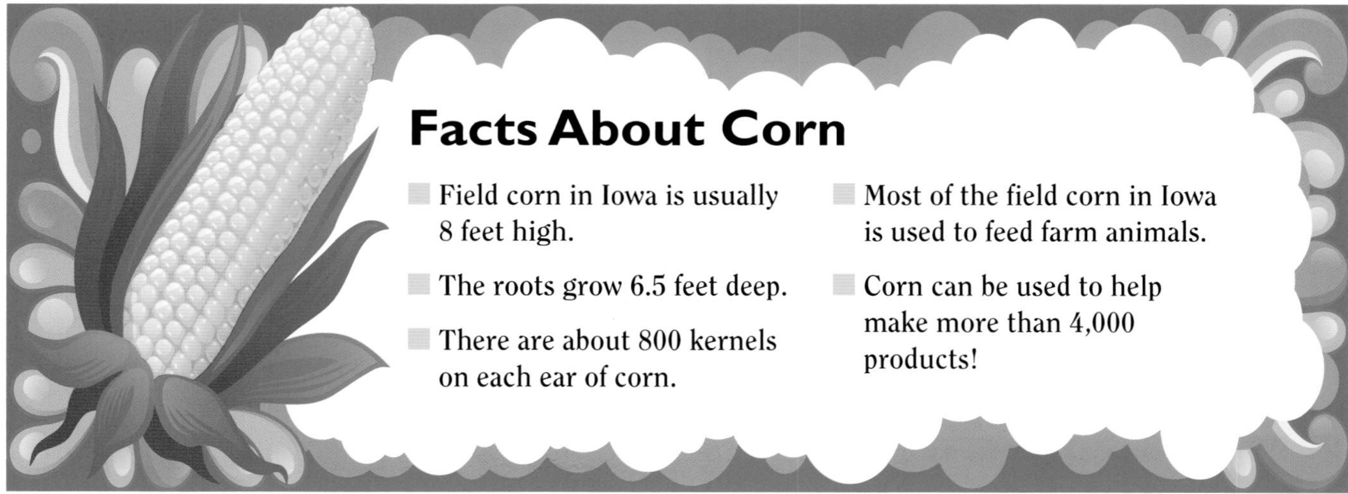

Facts About Corn

- Field corn in Iowa is usually 8 feet high.
- The roots grow 6.5 feet deep.
- There are about 800 kernels on each ear of corn.
- Most of the field corn in Iowa is used to feed farm animals.
- Corn can be used to help make more than 4,000 products!

Land of the Mound Builders

More than 2,000 years ago, a group of Mound builders lived along the Mississippi River. These Native Americans built mounds of dirt in the shapes of bears and birds. Archaeologists (scientists who study people of ancient times) think these mounds marked the burial spots of these people. The animal mounds may have been used to mark other ceremonies as well, not just burials. Today, you can still see more than 200 of these mounds. They are found at the Effigy Mound National Monument in northeastern Iowa.

FUN FACT President Harry S. Truman made the Effigy Mounds a national park on October 25, 1949.

Iowa State Capitol in Des Moines

Crack Open a Rock?

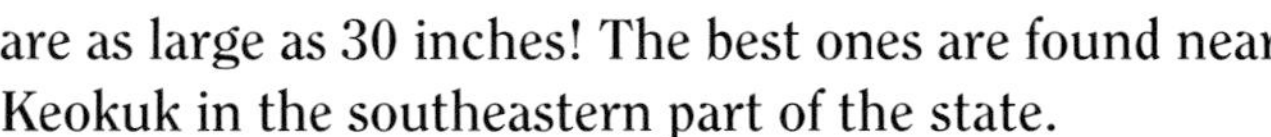

The geode is Iowa's state rock. On the outside, these rocks look like lumpy, normal rocks. They have a hard shell, but when you crack them open, you will find they are full of sparkling crystals. Most geodes are 2 to 6 inches wide. But some are as large as 30 inches! The best ones are found near Keokuk in the southeastern part of the state.

DID YOU KNOW?

Iowa is the only state whose name begins with two vowels.

Let's Bike!

Every summer, the *Des Moines Register* newspaper hosts a seven-day bicycle ride across Iowa. It is called Register's Annual Great Bike Ride Across Iowa. Bicyclists enjoy riding through the small towns along the way. They ride from the Missouri River on the western side of the state to the Mississippi River on the eastern side. The route is more than 450 miles! Children sometimes ride for part of the route with their parents.

Kansas

The name Kansas comes from the Sioux word *kansa,* which means "people of the wind." Kansas has wheat fields, grain elevators, small towns, and big cities. The Flint Hills run along the eastern part of the state. Wide plains cover the central part and the west. Kansas leads the nation in growing wheat. The state is also rich in oil, natural gas, zinc, coal, salt, and lead. People work in factories making trucks, trains, cars, airplanes, and computers.

STATE FACTS

Statehood: January 29, 1861—34th state
Capital: Topeka
Nickname: The Sunflower State
Motto: To the Stars Through Difficulty
State Bird: Western meadowlark

State Flower: Sunflower
State Tree: Cottonwood
State Animal: American Buffalo
State Song: "Home on the Range"

History of Kansas

This statue in Wichita is called "The Keeper of the Plains."

Plains Indians were some of the first people to live in this area. They belonged to the Kansa, Osage, Pawnee, and Wichita nations. In 1854, Kansas became a territory of the United States. At this time, the northern states did not allow slavery, but the southern states did. Would Kansas become a free state or a slave state? Because of the fighting over slavery, Kansas received the nickname "Bleeding Kansas."

In 1861, Kansas joined the Union as a free state. They did not allow slavery. After the Civil War, white and African Americans lived in Kansas. Almost 3 million people live in Kansas today. Many people live in the cities of Kansas City, Topeka, and Wichita.

Amber Waves of Grain

Kansas farmers grow more wheat than any other state. Most farmers in Kansas grow winter wheat. This wheat is planted in the fall, grown through winter, and harvested during the hot, windy days at the end of June. Farmers store the wheat in tall grain elevators found in almost every Kansas town. Farmers also raise beef cattle and grow soybeans and sorghum (a grain that is used to feed farm animals).

Famous Kansans

Amelia Earhart was born in Atchison, Kansas, in the northeastern part of the state. She was the first woman to fly alone across the Atlantic Ocean. She encouraged women to chase their goals. She disappeared on a 1937 flight when she tried to fly around the world.

Dwight Eisenhower was the 34th president of the United States. He grew up in Abilene, Kansas. During World War II, he was the commander of the Allied Forces in Europe.

Art on the Plains

The small town of Lindsborg, Kansas, is full of art galleries and studios. There you will see the work of painters, potters, woodcarvers, sculptors, and photographers. The town also celebrates its Swedish heritage. If you visit Lindsborg, look for the bright red wooden Dala horses. On Main Street, there's a Dala horse that looks big enough to ride!

FUN FACT Lindsborg was settled by Swedish immigrants in 1869. It is also known as "Little Sweden."

Costumed dancers celebrate at the Svensk Hyllningsfest Swedish festival in Lindsborg.

The Wild West

In the mid-1800s, the railroads built tracks through Kansas. Cowboys herded their cattle to stations in Abilene and Dodge City. After weeks of hard work along the cattle trails, the cowboys were ready for fun. Sometimes things got a little "wild." Lawmen including Wyatt Earp and Bat Masterson tried to keep law and order in the cattle towns.

The town of Lebanon, Kansas, is at the center of the continental United States (which does not include Alaska or Hawaii).

Michigan

Michigan is a state that has two pieces of land separated by water. Each piece is a peninsula (land that is surrounded by water on three sides). The Lower Peninsula looks like a giant mitten. Most of Michigan's cities and farms are found here. The farms grow cherries, apples, and dairy products. The Upper Peninsula is covered with lakes and pine forests. When fur trappers first came to this area, they trapped wolverines. Today, people come here to camp and fish.

Motor City

"Motor City" is a good nickname for Detroit. This city is the leader in making cars and trucks. It makes more cars and trucks than anywhere else in the United States. It all began with Henry Ford. In 1908, his company started building a car called the "Model T." Ford had invented a new, better way for people to work in factories. The new way was called the assembly line. Workers had to do only one job instead of many. This meant that workers at Ford factories could make cars faster and cheaper than anyone else. Making cars is still a major part of Michigan's economy. Many people in the Motor City area depend on these jobs.

The Ford Motor Company assembly line in 1916

Don't Touch Me!

What Great Lake does not touch the state of Michigan? Lakes Erie, Huron, Michigan, and Superior touch Michigan. Lake Ontario is the only Great Lake that does not touch the Great Lakes State.

Mobile in Mackinac

Believe it or not, Michigan has an island that does not allow cars or trucks. This island is Mackinac Island. The only way to get there is by ferryboat or plane. On the island, people have to walk, bike, or ride in horse-drawn carriages. If you go to Mackinac Island, be sure to visit the shops and sample the fudge. (People say that the marshmallows are the best!)

FUN FACT Houses on Mackinac Island do not have mailboxes. People who live there must go to the post office to pick up their mail.

DID YOU KNOW?

Michigan's name comes from two Chippewa words, *mici* and *gama*, which mean "great lake."

Morning Meals

More than 100 years ago, Dr. John Kellogg wanted his patients to eat healthy food. So he and his brother, Will, invented a breakfast food called "corn flakes." Will started a company that made cereal. One of Dr. Kellogg's patients liked the corn flakes so much that he started his own cereal company too. His name was Charles William Post. Their companies grew to be really big. Today, Kellogg's and Post cereals are still made in Battle Creek, Michigan. This city makes more breakfast cereal than any other city in the world. It is known as the "Cereal Bowl of America!"

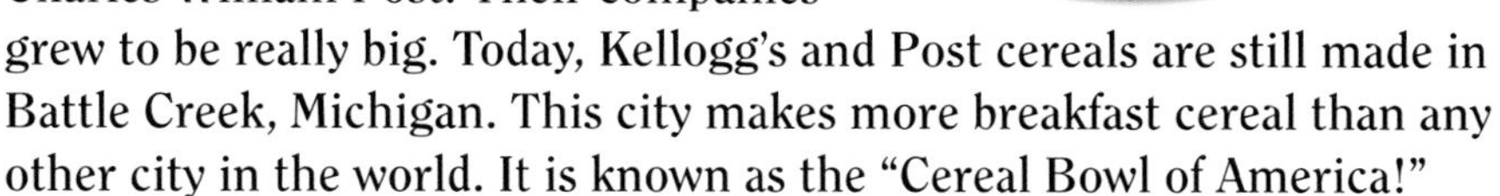

STATE FACTS

Statehood: January 26, 1837—26th state

Capital: Lansing

Nickname: The Wolverine State

Motto: If You Seek a Peninsula, Look About You

State Bird: Robin

State Flower: Apple blossom

McIntosh Mills

Michigan is famous for apples, especially the McIntosh apple. There are many cider mills in Michigan. Cider is made from apples. Some of these cider mills are more than 100 years old. One of these old mills is in Franklin, Michigan. Visitors come here to watch apples being pressed into cider.

Minnesota

More than five million people live in Minnesota. Many residents live in the Twin Cities of Minneapolis and St. Paul. Farming is important in the southern and western parts of the state. Minnesota leads the nation in growing green peas, sweet corn, and sugar beets. Farmers also grow corn, soybeans, and wheat. The Mesabi Range is in the northeastern part of Minnesota. Here, workers dig out iron ore and taconite (a rock that has iron ore in it) from the ground.

STATE FACTS

Statehood: May 11, 1858—32nd state
Capital: St. Paul
Nickname: Land of 10,000 Lakes
Motto: The Star of the North
State Bird: Common loon

State Flower: Pink and white lady slipper
State Tree: Norway pine
State Fish: Walleye
State Grain: Northern wild rice
State Sport: Hockey

Who Lives in Minnesota?

The land of Minnesota first belonged to Native Americans. They were the Nakota, Dakota, Lakota, Cree, Anishinabe, and Cheyenne. During the 1860s, the Unites States government pushed these people off their lands. At the same time, people from Germany, Sweden, and Norway began to settle this land. Today, people from Southeast Asia and east Africa live in Minnesota. About 68,000 Native Americans still live in Minnesota. Many are from the Anishinabe nation.

DID YOU KNOW?

International Falls, Minnesota, is the coldest place in the continental United States.

Land of Lakes

Minnesota is called the "Land of 10,000 Lakes." (Actually, there are more than 11,000 lakes.) They are an important part of Minnesota's recreation. In the summer, many Minnesotans go to these lakes to fish, boat, water ski, and relax at their cabins. In the winter, the temperatures drop and snow falls. But many Minnesotans still like to be outside. They play hockey, snowmobile, cross-country ski, and ice fish on the frozen lakes.

Northern Wildlife

Common Loon

Moose

Minnesota is full of northern wildlife. Loons, bald eagles, moose, grey wolves, northern pike, and porcupines live on this land. Here are some fun things to know about some of the wild animals of Minnesota: The grey wolf has a sense of smell that is 100 times stronger than a human. The porcupine eats almost anything, including canoe paddles and axe handles! The loon makes a noise that sounds like a strange cry. A moose can run up to 35 miles per hour!

Grey Wolf

Porcupine

Minnesota Mascots

The Twin Cities of Minneapolis and St. Paul have many professional sports teams. The Vikings are the football team. The Timberwolves are the basketball team. The Wild are the hockey team. And the Twins are the baseball team.

FUN FACT The Twins baseball cap has the letters T and C. They stand for Twin Cities.

Sugar Beets

Farmers in northwestern Minnesota grow sugar beets. But don't try to eat them! They are bigger than softballs and harder than rocks. Sugar beets are ground into sugar in factories before they can be used as food.

Visit Paul Bunyan and Babe

Statues of Paul Bunyan and Babe, his blue ox, are in Bemidji. The tale of Paul Bunyan is a made-up story about a very large lumberjack, a person who cuts down trees.

Missouri

The state of Missouri is in the middle of the United States. It is home to the two largest rivers in the country: the Missouri River and the Mississippi River. These rivers meet just north of the city of St. Louis. The explorers Lewis and Clark began their famous expedition (trip) near St. Louis. From 1803 to 1806, they explored the Missouri River and the land to the west.

STATE FACTS

Statehood: August 10, 1821—24th state

Capital: Jefferson City

Nickname: The "Show-Me" State

Motto: Let the Welfare of the People Be the Supreme Law

State Bird: Bluebird

State Tree: Flowering dogwood

State Musical Instrument: Fiddle

DID YOU KNOW?

The state animal of Missouri is a mule.

Missouri Life

Almost six million people live in Missouri today. In the north, farmers grow corn and soybeans. They raise cattle and hogs. The big cities of Kansas City and St. Louis are on opposite sides of the state. Kansas City has livestock markets. St. Louis is known for banking, as well as making metal. The southern part of Missouri is full of woods, lakes, hills, rivers, and small farms. Many people go to Branson to hear concerts. Other visitors enjoy the Lake of the Ozarks where they boat and fish.

Gateway to the West

The St. Louis Gateway Arch is the country's tallest monument. It was built from 1963 to 1965. It is 630 feet tall and 630 feet wide at the base. It weighs almost 35 million pounds! If you go to the Arch, you can ride a tram to the top. The Arch is part of the Jefferson National Expansion Memorial. It honors President Thomas Jefferson and all who helped settle the west. It also honors Dred Scott. He was a slave who fought for his freedom in the St. Louis Courthouse.

Land of Beginnings

Lewis and Clark began their trip to claim the Northwest Territory in Missouri, but they were not the only ones to begin an adventure here. Many settlers also began their journeys in Missouri. What trails began in the state of Missouri? The Santa Fe Trail began in St. Louis, Missouri. The Oregon Trail began in Independence, Missouri. Pioneers stocked up with supplies in these towns and traveled across the country.

Mark Twain

Mark Twain was an American author who grew up in Hannibal, Missouri. This small town is on the shores of the Mississippi River. When he was an adult, he wrote *The Adventures of Tom Sawyer* and *The Adventures of Huckleberry Finn*. These books are based on some of his boyhood adventures. They also help readers understand how African Americans were treated and what life was like on the Mississippi River. Today, you can visit Hannibal to see the Mark Twain Museum. There you will learn many things about Mark Twain, such as what his real name is: Samuel Langhorne Clemens.

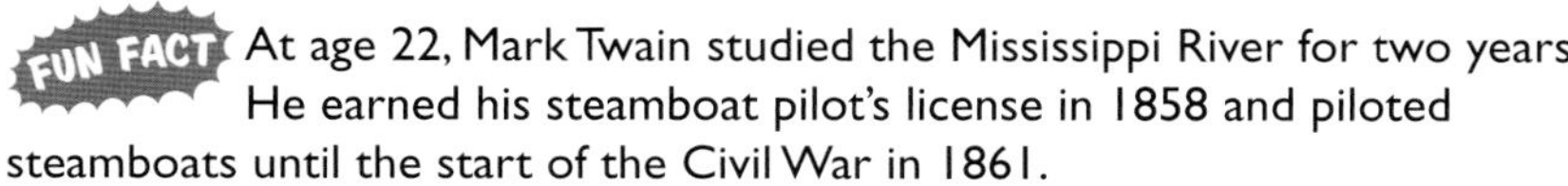

FUN FACT At age 22, Mark Twain studied the Mississippi River for two years. He earned his steamboat pilot's license in 1858 and piloted steamboats until the start of the Civil War in 1861.

Missouri and the Civil War

Missouri's location played a part in its role in the Civil War. Many Southerners had settled in the area and brought slaves with them. Nearby were states with many people who believed that slavery should be outlawed.

1821	As part of the Missouri Compromise, Missouri enters the Union as a slave state.
1854	Fighting begins between anti-slavery Kansas and pro-slavery Missouri.
1857	United States Supreme Court rules that Dred Scott, a Missouri slave, does not have rights as a citizen.
March 1861	Missouri votes to stay in the Union and remain neutral if war starts.
April through August 1861	Missouri refuses to send troops to fight for the Union. Union soldiers fight the Missouri state militia and are defeated.
October 1861	Missouri decides to join the Confederacy.

Nebraska

The name Nebraska comes from the Otoe Indian word *nebrathka,* which means "flat river." This describes the Platte River. It is flat, wide, and very shallow. Most of Nebraska's people live in the eastern part of the state near Omaha and Lincoln. The Sandhills cover much of western Nebraska. Farm animals graze on the grass that grows on the sandy soil of the Sandhills.

STATE FACTS

Statehood: March 1, 1867—37th state
Capital: Lincoln
Nickname: The Cornhusker State
Motto: Equality Before the Law
State Bird: Western meadowlark
State Flower: Goldenrod

Indian Lands of Nebraska

Long ago, Native Americans lived on the land that is now Nebraska. They belonged to the Omaha, Otoe, Pawnee, Ponca, and Arapaho nations. But during the 19th century, this changed. The United States government made the Native Americans give up their land and move to reservations. By 1854, the United States government opened the Nebraska Territory. Thousands of white settlers came to Nebraska and made it their new home.

Nebraska became a state in 1867. The Native American Chief Crazy Horse and his people continued to fight to keep their lands. But in 1877, they surrendered near Fort Robinson. Very few of Nebraska's people are Native Americans today.

Nebraska State Capitol in Lincoln

Free to Build a Home

In 1862, President Abraham Lincoln signed the Homestead Act. That meant people could get free land! Thousands of settlers moved to Nebraska to get their share of the land. It wasn't easy. Insects, blizzards, dust storms, and lack of water made farming difficult. Because there were few trees on the plains, many settlers built houses made of sod with grass roofs. Today, people can visit the first home built from the Homestead Act. It is near Beatrice, Nebraska, at the National Homestead Monument.

Hello, Cranes

Nebraska is in the middle of the Central Flyway. This is one of the best places in the country for bird watchers. Every spring, about 500,000 Sandhill cranes land on the shores of the shallow Platte River. They rest here and eat before flying north. Sandhill cranes are large birds. They are 3 to 4 feet tall and have wingspans of 5 to 6 feet. If you are in Nebraska in the springtime, listen. You may hear the sound of their haunting calls.

FUN FACT Along with the Sandhill cranes, more than 10 million ducks, geese, and other birds fly through the Central Flyway every year.

The Helpful Cottonwood

The cottonwood is the state tree of Nebraska. Cottonwoods grow best in moist soil. Pioneers who came to Nebraska knew water would be near cottonwood trees. They also used the trees to build their houses. These trees still grow in many parts of Nebraska. In early summer, the wind blows the "cotton" fluff that carries their seeds. The fluff looks like feathers or snow.

DID YOU KNOW?

Nebraska has more miles of river than any other state.

Chimney Rock

In the 1800s, pioneers who crossed Nebraska on the Oregon Trail saw an odd-shaped rock formation. They used this as a landmark to know they were traveling in the right direction along the trail. The rock formation rises 325 feet from the North Platte River valley. It is called Chimney Rock because of its pointy shape at the top. The area around Chimney Rock was made into a National Historic site on August 9, 1956. You can also see Chimney Rock on Nebraska's state quarter.

North Dakota

North Dakota is full of rolling plains and rich soil. This state grows more barley, sunflower seeds, and durum wheat than any other state. The western part of the state has large amounts of oil. People think that wind energy will be the new big business in North Dakota. This state may be large, but the number of people who live here is small. Only two states (Wyoming and Vermont) have fewer people than North Dakota.

STATE FACTS

Statehood: November 2, 1889—39th or 40th state (shared with South Dakota)

Capital: Bismarck

Nickname: The Peace Garden State

Motto: Liberty and Union Now and Forever, One and Inseparable

State Bird: Western meadowlark

State Flower: Wild prairie rose

State Honorary Equine: Nokota horse

State Fruit: Chokecherry

Mandan Kindness

In 1804, President Thomas Jefferson asked Meriwether Lewis and William Clark to explore the Missouri River. Lewis and Clark agreed. When winter arrived, they were in present-day North Dakota. The weather was cold. The Mandan people allowed Lewis and Clark to stay in their village until springtime. When the weather became warmer, the explorers followed the Missouri River to the west.

William Clark

Meriwether Lewis

Peace to All!

The International Peace Garden is located on North Dakota's border with Canada. It was made to honor the friendship between the two nations. The garden has more than 100,000 flowers. Some of the flowers are planted to look like flags of the United States and Canada. The Peace Garden also has seven "peace poles." The phrase "May Peace Prevail" is written in 28 different languages.

FUN FACT In 1957, people in North Dakota voted to nickname their state the Peace Garden State because of the International Peace Garden.

Extreme Weather!

North Dakota is a land of extremes. The record high temperature is 121 degrees. The record low is 60 degrees below zero! North Dakota's winters feel extra cold because of the strong winds and blowing snow. When blizzards hit, it is impossible to travel. Drifts of snow cover the roads. In spring, the Red River and the James River often flood because of the melting snow. But most summers are beautiful. The sun and the wind make the summer days warm and breezy.

Can Badlands Be Beautiful?

The eastern part of North Dakota is farmland. The western part is rangeland (land where herd animals graze). North Dakota also has a surprise: The Badlands! The Badlands are rock formations that were shaped by wind and water. The rocks have colorful bands of purple, rust, and red.

In 1883, Theodore Roosevelt lived in the Badlands and ranched. During this time, he saw the need to take care of nature. When he became president, he formed many national parks and forests.

DID YOU KNOW?

When President Harrison signed the papers for North and South Dakota, he shuffled them so that neither state could say they were admitted to the Union ahead of the other.

Let's Have a Powwow

The lands of North Dakota have a proud Native American history. Every year, Native Americans from more than 70 nations come to Bismarck, North Dakota, to celebrate a powwow. There are more than 1,500 dancers and drummers at the powwow and more than 20,000 people come to see the event. The United Tribes International Powwow is held at the Lone Star Arena.

Ohio

Ohio gets its name from the Ohio River. The Iroquois people called it *o-HY-o,* which means "great river" or "something great." The Ohio River forms the state's southern border. The land in Ohio is also pretty great. It is good for growing soybeans, corn, and tomatoes. Farmers here raise hogs, cattle, and poultry. The land is hilly in southern Ohio. These are the foothills of the Appalachian Mountains.

STATE FACTS:

Statehood: March 1, 1803—17th state
Capital: Columbus
Nickname: The Buckeye State
Motto: With God All Things Are Possible
State Bird: Cardinal
State Flower: Carnation
State Tree: Buckeye

The Flag Tells All

Ohio's flag describes the state. The blue triangle is for Ohio's hills and valleys. The red and white stripes are for Ohio's roads and waterways. The white circle is for the buckeye and the O in Ohio. The 17 stars are for Ohio's statehood, since Ohio became the 17th state in 1803.

Who Lives in Ohio?

Thousands of years ago, mound-building Native Americans lived on the land that is now Ohio. Later, people from the Iroquois nation lived on the land. Ohio became a state in 1803. People moved here from other countries. Many people from Germany farmed and worked in the steel mills. People from Ireland worked on the canals that helped move goods across the state. During World War I, many African Americans came to Ohio from the south. They found jobs and made better lives for their families in Ohio. Today, more than 11 million people live in Ohio.

This mound is in Hopewell Culture National Park.

What's a Buckeye?

Ohio's state tree is the buckeye. These trees have prickly shelled fruits that are a little bigger than a golf ball. If you peel off the outer shell, you will find a smooth, dark brown nut with a tan spot. It looks like an eye of a buck, or male deer. Buckeye trees grow throughout the state of Ohio. People from Ohio call themselves "buckeyes."

FUN FACT Native Americans would roast, peel, and mash buckeye nuts and add them to healthy meals. Some people carry the buckeye nut as a lucky charm.

Famous Ohioans

Ohio is famous for its pilots and astronauts.

Judith Resnik was one of the first female astronauts. She was a mission specialist on the Space Shuttle *Discovery* in 1984. But there was an accident in 1986. The Space Shuttle *Challenger* exploded during the launch. Resnik, along with all the other astronauts, died in the accident. Resnik was born in Akron, Ohio.

On July 1969, **Neil Armstrong** became the first person to walk on the moon. He was the commander of the *Apollo 11* space mission. Armstrong was born in Wapakoneta, Ohio. If you go to Wapakoneta today, you can visit the Neil Armstrong Air and Space Museum.

DID YOU KNOW?

Ohio is known as the "Mother of Presidents" because eight presidents were born in this state.

1. **William H. Harrison**
2. **Ulysses S. Grant**
3. **Rutherford B. Hayes**
4. **James Garfield**
5. **Benjamin Harrison**
6. **William McKinley**
7. **William Howard Taft**
8. **Warren G. Harding**

Rock on Cleveland!

If you want to see a new kind of museum, go to Cleveland. Instead of paintings, fossils, or science exhibits, this museum has music, costumes, and instruments. It is the Rock and Roll Hall of Fame and Museum, and it tells the history of rock music. Visitors can listen to music and watch concert videos. Cleveland might seem like a strange place for a rock and roll museum, but the city is part of rock history. In 1951, a Cleveland radio disc jockey made up the term *rock and roll*. In 1952, Cleveland hosted the first rock concert.

South Dakota

South Dakota is made up of many different types of land. It has prairies, glacial lakes, farmland, rangeland, the Badlands, and the Black Hills. South Dakota's economy also comes from different sources. Many people visit South Dakota for the beautiful and historic sites. Custer State Park has one of the largest bison herds in the nation. Each fall, it has a roundup! Farmers in South Dakota grow soybeans and corn. They raise beef cattle and sheep. Sioux Falls is South Dakota's biggest city.

STATE FACTS

Statehood: November 2, 1889—39th or 40th state (shared with North Dakota)
Capital: Pierre
Nickname: Mount Rushmore State
Motto: Under God the People Rule
State Bird: Chinese ring-necked pheasant
State Flower: Pasque flower
State Animal: Coyote
State Fossil: *Triceratops*
State Sport: Rodeo

Mount Rushmore

Mount Rushmore is South Dakota's most famous landmark. During the years 1927 to 1941, sculptor Gutzon Borglum carved the faces of four American presidents into the giant mountainside. This was his memorial to the United States and its government. The four presidents carved on Mount Rushmore are George Washington, Thomas Jefferson, Theodore Roosevelt, and Abraham Lincoln.

Gutzon Borglum

FUN FACT Most of the carving was done with dynamite. Workers blasted nearly one billion pounds of rock off Mount Rushmore.

Native American History

South Dakota is home to the Lakota, Dakota, and Nakota Indians, which make up the Sioux nation. The history of these people has been painful. In 1868, the Fort Laramie Treaty said that the Black Hills belonged to the Lakota people. But in 1874, gold was discovered in the hills. Miners and settlers rushed into the area. In 1876, the United States government forced the Native Americans out of the Black Hills. They were made to live on reservations. Today, South Dakota has eight reservations. But Native Americans do not have to live on reservations. As American citizens, they may live wherever they choose.

Corn Murals

The Corn Palace is located in Mitchell, South Dakota. Each year, new murals made of different-colored corn and grasses decorate the walls of the palace. In the summer, the Corn Palace welcomes visitors. During the rest of the year, it is used for basketball games, graduations, and even the high school prom.

Mining for Gold

Gold was discovered in the Black Hills in 1874. Many people moved to the town of Deadwood to mine for gold. In 1877, the Homestake Gold Mine opened in the nearby town of Lead. It became one of the biggest gold mines in the United States. In 2002, the gold mine closed. It had been open for 125 years! Soon it will be used as an underground lab to study science.

Deadwood, South Dakota

DID YOU KNOW?

The USS *South Dakota* was the most decorated battleship during World War II.

A Dinosaur Named Sue

In 1990, a paleontologist (a scientist who studies fossils) named Sue Hendrickson made a huge discovery. She found the remains of a *Tyrannosaurus rex* that was almost 67 million years old. It was found near the Cheyenne River Indian Reservation in South Dakota. It is the largest and most complete fossil of a dinosaur ever found. The dinosaur can be seen today at the Field Museum of Natural History in Chicago, Illinois. The dinosaur is named Sue.

Wisconsin

Wisconsin is nestled between the state of Minnesota and Lake Michigan. It has forests, fields, rivers, steep bluffs, and more than 25,000 miles of snowmobile trails. More than one million cows are raised in this state, which is why Wisconsin is known across the nation as "America's Dairyland." Wisconsin also makes farm tools, metal products, and machinery.

STATE FACTS

Statehood: May 29, 1848—30th state
Capital: Madison
Nickname: The Badger State
Motto: Forward
State Bird: American robin

State Flower: Wood violet
State Dog: American water spaniel
State Mineral: Galena

Wisconsin is America's Dairyland.

Wisconsin History

The Menominee, Winnebago, and Dakota Indians were some of the first people to live in Wisconsin. In 1634, fur traders from France and England began to explore the area. The first settlers came to Wisconsin in the 1820s because of a lead-mining boom. Later, the United States government fought the Native Americans. They forced them off their land.

Wisconsin became a state in 1848. Many settlers wanted a good education for their children. They built schools and universities. Now, more than five million people live in the state. Milwaukee is Wisconsin's largest city.

DID YOU KNOW?

In 1856, the first kindergarten in the country opened in Watertown, Wisconsin.

The Badger State

Badgers are fierce animals with strong claws. They use their claws to dig burrows for their homes. In Wisconsin, people were called "badgers." The nickname started in the 1820s in the southwestern part of the state. Miners dug tunnels in the hills when they looked for lead. Some of them lived in these tunnels in the winter, just like badgers. The badger nickname was given to all people who live in Wisconsin. Today, Wisconsin is known as the Badger State.

Cheese Quiz

Wisconsin produces more cheese than any other state. Each year, 15,000 farms produce milk for making cheese. It takes about ten pounds of milk to make one pound of cheese. How many pounds of cheese are made in Wisconsin each year? 2.6 billion pounds—that's a lot of cheese!

FUN FACT People from Wisconsin call themselves "cheeseheads." You can see Green Bay Packer football fans wear foam cheesehead hats at their home football games.

Come to the Circus!

Five brothers from the Ringling family started a circus in 1884 in Baraboo, Wisconsin. Because they didn't have much money, they did all the work and performances. Soon they became famous in Wisconsin and across the country. By 1910, they needed 92 railway cars to move all of the animals and performers. Today, you can visit the Circus World Museum in Baraboo, Wisconsin.

Shaped by Ice

Thousands of years ago, Wisconsin was covered by a glacier—a great sheet of ice. As the glacier melted, it changed the land. The glacier left behind these land forms:

kettle: a round pond

moraine: a pile of dirt and rock

drumlin: an oval-shaped hill of rock

esker: a trail of sand and gravel formed by rivers running under the melting glacier

This kettle is in Kettle Moraine Forest.

South

The land of the South starts on the east coast. Eight southern states share a coastline with the Atlantic Ocean and Gulf of Mexico. The land crosses the Appalachian Mountains and stretches across hills and fields to the middle of the United States. Much of the South is surrounded by water. The Ohio River flows on the northern side of the region. The mighty Mississippi River streams near the region's western edge. A large body of water called the Gulf of Mexico sits to the south.

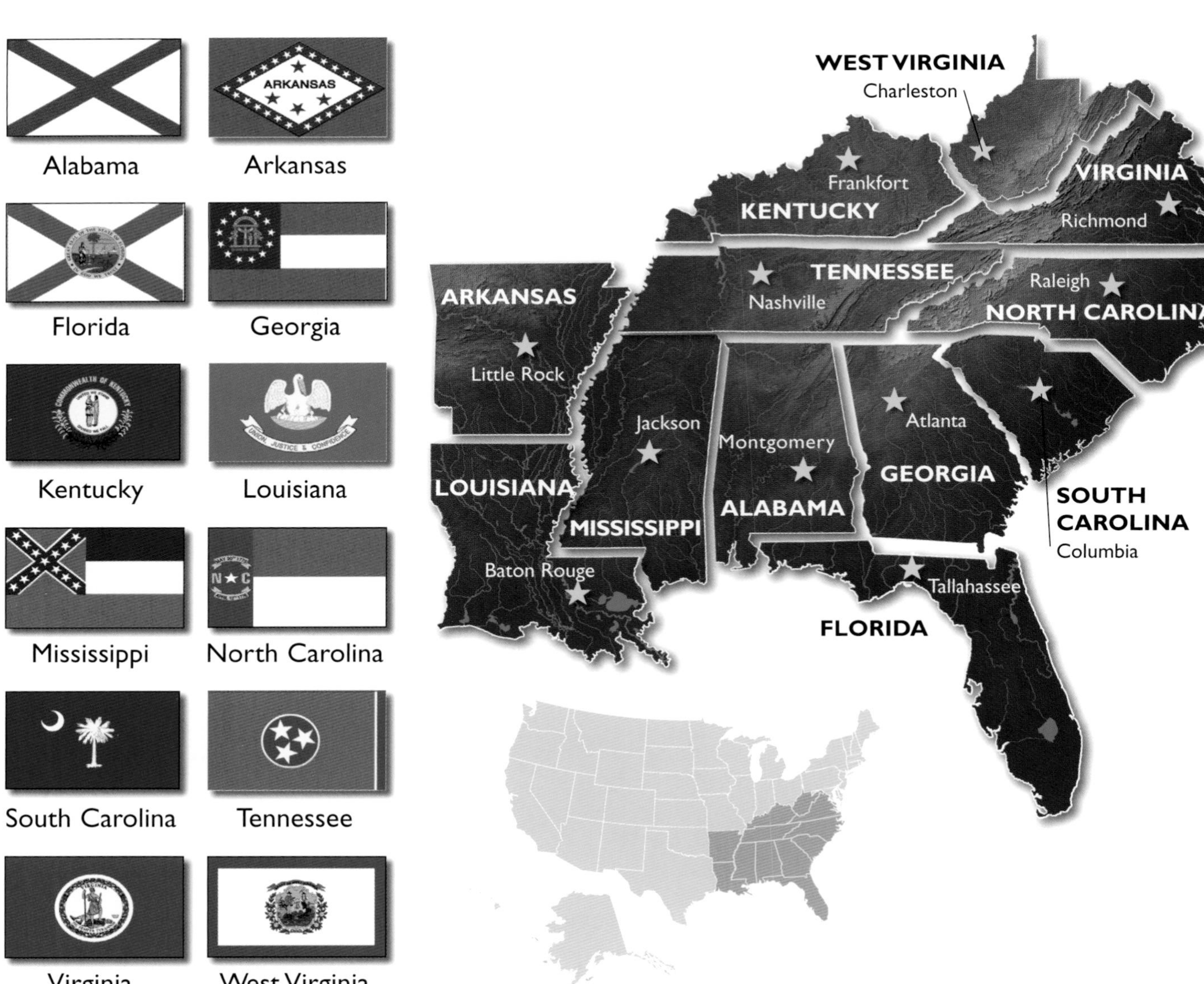

Southern Living

The warm climate allows southerners to live off the land. Farmers grow cotton, tobacco, rice, corn, and soybeans. People use the land's natural resources to make products, such as cloth and furniture. Cities in the South are growing. Charlotte, North Carolina, is becoming a center for banks. Atlanta, Georgia, has the busiest airport in the country.

Civil War to Civil Rights

Sculpture of Southern Civil War leaders in Stone Mountain, Georgia

Long ago, plantation owners in the South forced African slaves to do the farm work. When people from the North tried to end slavery in the 1860s, some of the Southern states rebelled. Eleven states broke away from the Union. They formed a new country called the Confederate States of America. During the Civil War, the North fought the South over slavery and whether America would remain one nation or break into two countries. The South lost, and slavery came to an end.

Statue of Martin Luther King Jr. in Alabama

The Southern states rejoined the United States, but African Americans were still not given fair treatment. Some laws segregated (separated) blacks from whites. This made it hard for them to vote or get a good education. During the 1950s and 1960s, African Americans and others worked together for civil rights. Martin Luther King Jr. was one of the leaders in the civil rights movement.

Songs of the South

The South is known for its music. Jazz music began in New Orleans. Bluegrass music started in Kentucky. Elvis Presley was a singer born in Tupelo, Mississippi, and lived in Memphis, Tennessee. He will always be remembered for his style of Rock 'n' Roll. Nashville, Tennessee, is the center of country music.

Alabama

Alabama was named after the Alibamu Indians. The state has beautiful mountains to the north. To the south, Alabama borders the Gulf of Mexico. Cotton, peanuts, and corn are the state's major crops. People work in factories making iron and steel. Alabama is a growing center for car making. About 4.7 million people live in Alabama. Many people live in the cities of Birmingham, Montgomery, Mobile, and Huntsville.

STATE FACTS

Statehood: December 14, 1819—22nd state
Capital: Montgomery
Nickname: The Yellowhammer State
Motto: We Dare Maintain Our Rights
State Bird: Yellowhammer

State Flower: Camellia
State Reptile: Alabama red-bellied turtle
State Saltwater Fish: Fighting tarpon
State Freshwater Fish: Large-mouth bass

Cotton grows in a field in Alabama.

DID YOU KNOW?

Almost 83 million years ago, a meteorite landed near Wetumpka, Alabama. The crater it made is about five miles wide!

Heart of Dixie

During the Civil War, the city of Montgomery was the first capital of the Confederacy. It was also the capital of Alabama. The Confederate States of America were the 11 Southern states that left the Union in 1860 and 1861. Jefferson Davis became the Confederate president. He took the oath of office on February 18, 1861, on the steps of the capitol in Montgomery. The Confederate flag was flown for the first time over the capitol on March 4, 1861. Because of how important it has been in the history of the South and the Civil War, Alabama is nicknamed the "Heart of Dixie."

Hooray for A . . . and All of Alabama

Alabama is named for the Alibamu Indians.

Lake Guntersville is Alabama's largest lake.

Alabama's state flower is the camellia.

Birmingham is Alabama's largest city.

Alabama's state bird is the yellowhammer, a kind of woodpecker.

Montgomery is the capital of Alabama.

Alabama's nicknames include the Cotton State, Yellowhammer State, and the Heart of Dixie.

Bug Hero!

In the early 1900s, an insect called the boll weevil destroyed most of Alabama's cotton crop. Farmers were forced to grow other crops, such as peanuts. This turned out to be good news. Farmers started making more money with the new crops than they had with cotton. Alabama farmers would not have learned this without the boll weevil.

FUN FACT In 1919, the people of Enterprise, Alabama, built a statue to honor the boll weevil.

Sitting Down to Take a Stand

The civil rights movement began in Montgomery, Alabama. In December 1955, African American Rosa Parks refused to give up her bus seat to a white man. After she was arrested, Martin Luther King Jr. asked all African Americans to stop riding the buses in Montgomery. This was a peaceful way to bring attention to the problem. A year later, the United States Supreme Court ruled that segregating (separating) people on buses because of skin color was against the Constitution. These events would lead the nation to fight for equal rights for all citizens.

Sweet Home Alabama

These famous people were born in Alabama.

Mae Jemison
doctor and astronaut

Jesse Owens
Olympic track-and-field athlete

Hank Williams
country music star

Helen Keller
writer and educator

Joe Louis
boxer

Hank Aaron
baseball player

Arkansas

Arkansas is nicknamed the Natural State. It is a beautiful place for fishing, hiking, and being outdoors. Arkansas has two small mountain ranges: the Ozark Mountains and the Ouachita Mountains. The eastern part of Arkansas is flat and fertile. Farmers grow rice, cotton, and soybeans. The weather in Arkansas is exciting but can be dangerous. Thunderstorms and tornadoes come through in the warm months. Ice storms hit Arkansas in the winter.

STATE FACTS

Statehood: June 15, 1836—25th state
Capital: Little Rock
Nickname: The Natural State
Motto: The People Rule
State Bird: Mockingbird

State Flower: Apple blossom
State Tree: Pine
State Gem: Diamond
State Mineral: Quartz crystal

DID YOU KNOW?

Arkansas was the name that early French explorers made up for the Quapaw Indians. It means "south wind."

For North and South?

During the Civil War in the 1860s, some Arkansans wanted to leave the Union and join the South. Others wanted to stay in the Union. The state ended up joining the Confederacy of the South. When the Union Army took over northern Arkansas in 1863, Arkansas Confederates gathered in the southwest Arkansas town of Washington. The Union Army took over Little Rock. Arkansas remained divided until the end of the Civil War.

Little Rock's Brave Students

Years ago, black and white students were not allowed to go to the same schools. This was called segregation. In 1954, the United States government said that schools could no longer be segregated. In 1957, nine African American students tried to attend an all-white high school in Little Rock, Arkansas, but the governor of Arkansas stopped them. President Dwight Eisenhower stepped in and took action. He sent soldiers to Little Rock to protect the students so they could go to school. These students faced danger, but they helped end segregation. They are often called "The Little Rock Nine."

Free Diamonds!

Arkansas has diamonds! You can find them at the Crater of Diamonds State Park. It is the only place in the United States where diamonds are naturally found. Most of the diamonds are clear, yellow, or brown. You can also look for other rocks and minerals, such as jasper and garnet. Whatever diamonds you find are yours to keep! The Crater of Diamonds State Park is near Murfreesboro, Arkansas.

You're in Hot Water

Hot mineral water flows out of the slope of Hot Springs Mountain. This water helps people relax. It also helps ease pain. Years ago, Native Americans used these springs. During wartime, this was a neutral place. Native American warriors would rest in the hot springs in peace. Today, millions of people visit Hot Springs National Park. It has 47 hot springs that have temperatures of 143 degrees or more.

Native Americans called these springs the "Valley of the Vapors."

This is a rock formation inside a cave in Blachard Springs Cavern.

Famous Arkansas People

Bill Clinton
the 42nd president of the United States. He was born in the small town of Hope, Arkansas. He also lived in Little Rock, Arkansas.

Sam Walton
the founder of the Wal-Mart stores. He opened the first Wal-Mart in Rogers, Arkansas, in 1962. Today, Wal-Mart's main offices are in Bentonville, Arkansas.

Florida

Florida reaches the farthest south of any state on the mainland. It sticks out into the ocean, so it is surrounded by water on three sides. It is called the Sunshine State because of its warm weather and many beaches. At the tip of Florida, a string of tiny islands spread into the ocean. These are called the Florida Keys. The Panhandle is the northern part of the state that stretches west all the way to Alabama.

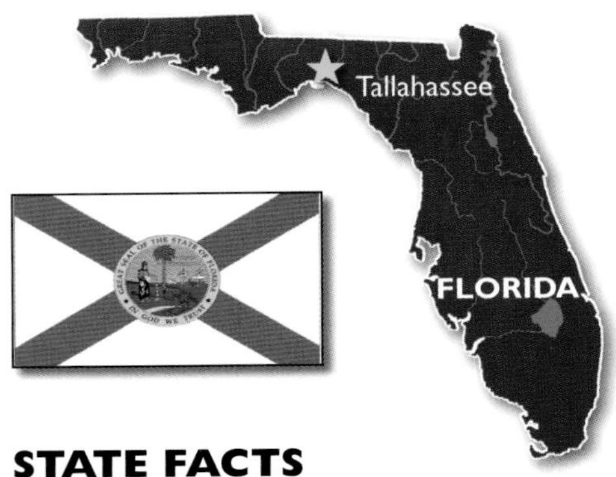

STATE FACTS

Statehood: March 3, 1845—27th state
Capital: Tallahassee
Nickname: The Sunshine State
Motto: In God We Trust
State Bird: Mockingbird

State Flower: Orange blossom
State Tree: Sabal palm

Vacation, Anyone?

Millions of people go to Florida for the warm sunshine, beautiful beaches, and amazing wildlife. They go to see the big attractions, such as Disney World, Epcot Center, and Universal Studios. Sea World has sea lions, dolphins, and exotic birds on display. But nothing beats the natural wildlife of Florida. Crystal River National Wildlife Refuge has manatees in their natural environment. Manatees are also called sea cows. An adult manatee can grow to be 12 feet long. It weighs up to 3,500 pounds!

Land Full of Flowers

In Spanish, Florida means "full of flowers." The Spanish were the first Europeans to reach Florida. In 1565, they built St. Augustine, the oldest city in the United States. If you visit this city, you can walk the narrow streets that were built hundreds of years ago!

Florida Then and Now

1513 A Spanish explorer lands on the Florida coast. His name is Juan Ponce de León.

1565 St. Augustine is founded. This is the first European settlement in the Americas.

1845 Florida becomes the 27th state on March 3.

1961 The first space flight with a human crew from America is launched from Cape Canaveral.

1971 Walt Disney World opens.

1992 Hurricane Andrew hits Florida.

Orange You Glad?

Florida grows more oranges than any other state. Each year, Florida grows 40 billion oranges. That's about eight oranges for each person on Earth. If all the oranges were lined up in a row, they would stretch to the moon and back four times! Oranges and orange blossoms are symbols of love.

Florida also grows more grapefruits and tangerines than any other state.

DID YOU KNOW?

During its long history, Florida has been a part of five different countries: Spain, France, Great Britain, the United States, and the Confederate States of America.

Wildlife of the Everglades

The Everglades is a 4,000-square-mile area of wetlands in southern Florida. A "prairie" of sawgrass grows on the swampy land. Many animals call this place their home. Look for the wildlife: ring-billed gulls (1), alligators (2), American crocodiles (3), wood storks (4), deer (5), great egrets (6), sandhill cranes (7), white ibises (8), Florida panthers (9), brown pelicans (10), and green turtles (11).

Georgia

Georgia is the largest southern state. In colonial times, forests and woodlands covered most of the land. In 1733, James Oglethorpe and a group of poor settlers arrived and named this colony Georgia, after King George II of England. Georgia leads the nation in growing peaches, peanuts, and pecans. It is known as the Peach State.

STATE FACTS

Statehood: January 2, 1788—4th state
Capital: Atlanta
Nickname: The Peach State
Motto: Wisdom, Justice, and Moderation
State Bird: Brown thrasher
State Flower: Cherokee rose

Savannah is home to many historic front-porch houses.

DID YOU KNOW?

The *City of Savannah* was the first steamship to cross the Atlantic Ocean. It sailed from Georgia.

Gems of Georgia

Georgia has been home to many famous people. Here are just a few:

Jimmy Carter
39th president of the United States

Ty Cobb
one of the greatest baseball players in history

Rebecca L. Felton
first female United States senator

Martin Luther King Jr.
African American minister and civil rights leader

Juliette Gordon Low
founder of the Girl Scouts of America

Jackie Robinson
first African American major-league baseball player

Margaret Mitchell
author of *Gone With the Wind*

Andrew Young
first African American ambassador to the United Nations

Hard-hitting History

During the Civil War, many battles were fought in Georgia. In 1864, General William Sherman led Union soldiers (the army of the North) to Atlanta. He set fire to the city, burning it to the ground. He marched on to Savannah, destroying railroads and burning crops along the way. After the war, the people of the south rebuilt Atlanta. Today, more than five million people live in the Atlanta area. Visitors come to see the historic buildings of the state.

A Rock the Size of a Mountain

Stone Mountain is a large dome rock the size of a mountain. It is near Atlanta, Georgia.

It is about 5 miles around its base and more than 1,600 feet tall. Stone Mountain is famous for its giant sculpture. It is one of the largest of its kind in the world. On one side of the rock there is a carving of Southern Civil War leaders. The sculpture shows Generals Robert E. Lee, Stonewall Jackson, Jefferson Davis, and their horses.

Something's Shaky

At the southeast corner of Georgia there is an area covered in tea-colored water. This is the Okefenokee Swamp. Its name comes from the Seminole Indian word that means "land of the trembling earth." They named it that because the swamp is made of floating islands, which shake when you walk on them. Thousands of plants and animals live there.

FUN FACT The water in the Okefenokee Swamp is dark brown and may look dirty, but it does not hurt the animals and fish in the swamp that drink it.

Nutty Facts

Peanuts are an important crop in Georgia. Here are some "nutty" facts:

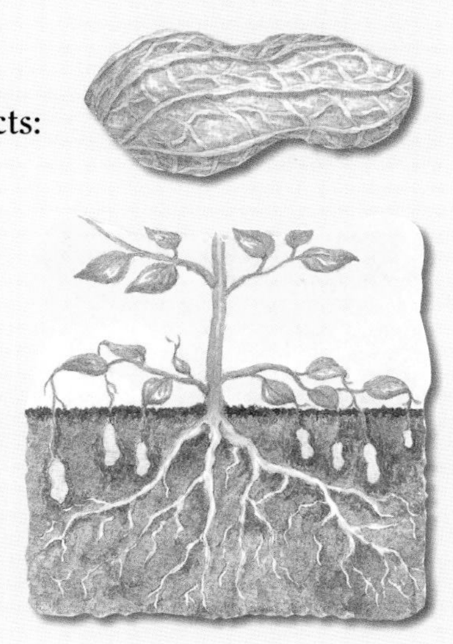

- A peanut is not a nut. It's a legume. It is related to a pea or a bean.
- A nickname for a peanut is a "goober" or a "goober pea." (Georgia is sometimes called the "Goober State.")
- Ground-up peanut shells are used to make wallboard, fireplace logs, and kitty litter.

Kentucky

The central part of Kentucky is covered with lush grass. Every spring, tiny blue blossoms bloom on the grass. This is why Kentucky is called the Bluegrass State. In eastern Kentucky, the Appalachian Mountains rise up from the land. They are covered with thick forests. The land becomes flat to the west. The Mississippi River flows along the western border.

Kentucky Progress

Settlers from the east wanted to move to Kentucky. But thick forests and the Appalachian Mountains were in the way. In 1750, Thomas Walker found a pass through the mountains. He called this pass the Cumberland Gap. About 30 years later, Daniel Boone and his woodsmen cleared a trail to the west called Wilderness Road, and they led many settlers into Kentucky. People liked this area because of its rich farmland and grasslands. Kentucky farmers now grow corn, soybeans, and tobacco. They raise chickens, goats, and cattle. In the cities, people work in factories making automobiles, refrigerators, and washing machines. People also work underground, mining coal.

STATE FACTS

Statehood: June 1, 1792—15th state
Capital: Frankfort
Nickname: The Bluegrass State
Motto: United We Stand, Divided We Fall
State Bird: Cardinal

State Flower: Goldenrod
State Horse: Thoroughbred
State Grass: Bluegrass
State Fish: Kentucky spotted bass
State Tree: Tulip poplar

Come Together

The state seal of Kentucky shows a pioneer in buckskin and a statesman shaking hands. It is a symbol of Kentucky's motto "United We Stand, Divided We Fall." It was chosen as the state seal in 1792. It is about the importance of coming together.

DID YOU KNOW?

Kentucky is from the Iroquois Indian word *ken-tah-ten*, which means "land of tomorrow."

This Cave Is Mammoth

The Mammoth Cave System is the longest system of caves in the world. It has five levels and more than 390 miles of passageways. Some rocks look like long straws. Others look like flowers or trees. Many rocks are brightly colored. The caves have lakes, rivers, and even waterfalls. They are home to many animals. With more than 28 trails for biking and walking, Mammoth Cave National Park is beautiful above the ground too.

A sculpture of a giant baseball bat stands outside the Louisville Slugger Musuem & Factory and Hillerich Bradsby Museum in Louisville.

Toe-tappin' Music

Bluegrass isn't just a name for Kentucky grass. It is also a style of music that began in Kentucky. It is sometimes called "mountain music." A bluegrass band uses fiddles, mandolins, guitars, banjos, and other stringed instruments. Bill Monroe was a famous bluegrass musician from Kentucky. His song "The Blue Moon of Kentucky" is the state's official bluegrass song.

Race Horses!

Kentucky is famous for its champion horses. Many of these horses are raised in the bluegrass region of central Kentucky. Each May, the most famous horse race in the country is held at Churchill Downs in Louisville. It's called the Kentucky Derby. The race is one and a quarter miles long. It is one of the oldest horse races in the United States.

The Kentucky Derby trophy is made of 56 ounces of 14- and 18-karat gold, and it is almost 2 feet tall!

Louisiana

Louisiana is shaped like a boot. The Mississippi River flows on the eastern side of the "boot." Then it flows through the "foot" of the boot into the Gulf of Mexico. Louisiana has many trees, lakes, swamps, and marshes. Most of the time the weather is hot and wet. Louisianans grow rice and cotton and drill for oil and gas. Many tourists come to Louisiana each year to visit the cities of New Orleans and Baton Rouge.

DID YOU KNOW?

The town of Jean Lafitte, Louisiana, was once a hide-away for pirates!

A bayou (swamp) in Louisiana

Double the Size!

In 1803, the United States extended west only to the Mississippi River. Then the United States bought a large area of land from France for $15 million. It was called the "Louisiana Purchase." This land stretched all the way to Canada and the Rocky Mountains. Louisiana and parts of 12 other states are in this area. It doubled the size of the United States. It also gave the United States full control of the Mississippi River.

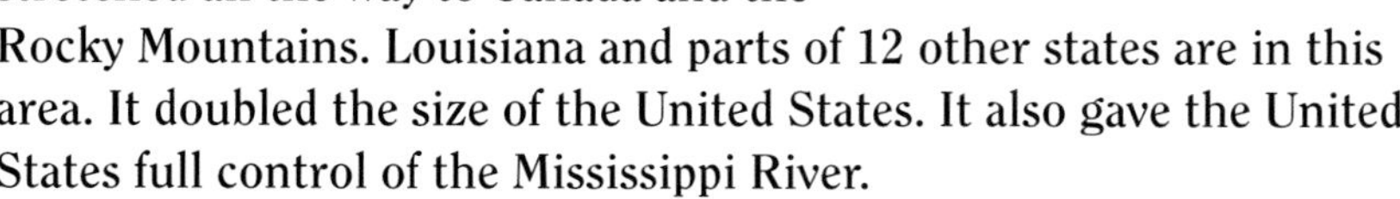

STATE FACTS

Statehood: April 30, 1812—18th state
Capital: Baton Rouge
Nickname: The Pelican State
Motto: Union, Justice, Confidence
State Bird: Eastern brown pelican

State Flower: Magnolia
State Musical Instrument: Diatonic accordion

Life of Louisiana

1682 Rene-Robert Cavelier, Sieur de la Salle, claims the Mississippi River valley for France and names it Louisiana.

1762 France gives Louisiana to Spain.

1800 Spain gives Louisiana back to France.

1803 The United States buys Louisiana from France.

1812 Louisiana becomes a state.

1861 Louisiana secedes (leaves) from the Union.

1868 Louisiana rejoins the United States.

2005 Hurricane Katrina hits Louisiana and floods the city of New Orleans.

Who Are the Cajuns?

Cajuns are a group of people who live in southern Louisiana. Their ancestors were French who settled in Canada in an area once called Acadia. In the 1700s, these "Acadians" moved to Louisiana. They became known as "Cajuns."

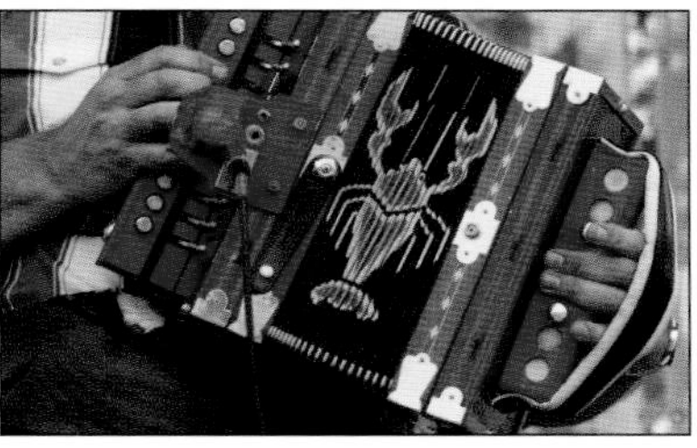

The Cajun language is a mix of French and English. Cajuns have their own special way of cooking. Their dishes use lots of Louisiana plants and animals, such as alligators, crawfish, turtles, shrimp, onions, tomatoes, okra, and hot peppers.

The city of Kaplan, Louisiana, is known as "The Most Cajun Place on Earth."

Look Where the Wind Blows

The people of Louisiana have faced many disasters. In 2005, Hurricane Katrina hit the shore of Louisiana. The floodwalls around New Orleans could not hold back the water. The city flooded. Many people had to leave the area, and others lost their homes. A few weeks later, Hurricane Rita hit Louisiana. More homes were damaged. The people of Louisiana are rebuilding New Orleans and the nearby towns and cities. People from across the United States are helping. Tourists are visiting New Orleans again.

The Brown Pelican

The Brown Pelican is the state bird of Louisiana. It is the only kind of pelican that dives from the sky to catch its food. About 50 years ago, the Brown Pelican almost disappeared. Chemicals in the water had harmed its eggs. Now they face new danger. In April 2010, oil spilled into the Gulf of Mexico. Scientists hope that the oil will not damage the places where the pelicans feed and nest.

The French Quarter in New Orleans is known for the style of its buildings, especially its iron-lace balconies.

Mississippi

Mississippi is in the deep south of the United States. This state took the name of the Mississippi River because it flows all along its western edge. The name comes from two Chippewa Indian words, *mici* and *zibi*, which mean "father of the waters." The waters of the river deposit rich, dark soil on the land. This soil is good for growing crops. The Piney Woods region covers the southern area of the state.

Jackson

MISSISSIPPI

STATE FACTS

Statehood: December 10, 1817—20th state

Capital: Jackson

Nickname: The Magnolia State

Motto: By Valor and Arms

State Bird: Mockingbird

State Flower: Magnolia blossom

State Fish: Largemouth bass

State Insect: Honeybee

DID YOU KNOW?

About half of all the people in Mississippi live in the country or in small towns.

Mighty Mississippi

1500
Choctaw, Chickasaw, and Natchez Indians live in Mississippi.

Spaniard Hernando de Soto is one of the first Europeans to see the Mississippi River.

1699
The French build the first European settlement in Mississippi.

1817
Mississippi becomes a state.

1837–38
Choctaw and Chickasaw Indians leave the state, some by force.

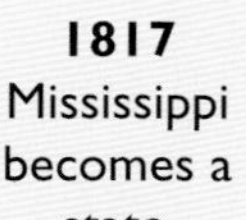

1861
Mississippi secedes (leaves) from the Union.

1870
Mississippi rejoins the United States.

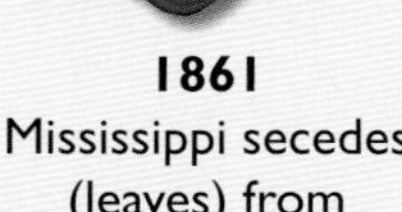

1964
A court orders Mississippi to put all races together in its schools.

Mississippi History

In the early 1800s, cotton was the major crop of Mississippi. White planters used African slaves to work the fields. In 1861, Mississippi became the second state to secede (leave) from the Union. After the Civil War, all slaves were free. But laws still kept African Americans segregated (separated) from whites. These laws were called "Jim Crow" laws. In the 1960s, African Americans fought for their civil rights. Mississippi was one of the battlegrounds. Many civil rights protests were held in Mississippi. Today, people of Mississippi are working together to improve their state.

People protested Jim Crow laws in 1961.

Southern Authors

Mississippi has a rich history of famous authors (writers). Many have written about the life and times of the South. Here are a few of them:

William Faulkner
born in New Albany, Mississippi

Eudora Welty
born in Jackson, Mississippi

Richard Wright
born on the Rucker Plantation in Roxie, Mississippi

Watch for Wildlife

Mississippi is full of wildlife. These animals are found within the state: wild boars, alligators, black bears, wild turkeys, and gopher tortoises. The black bear and the gopher tortoise are endangered species in Mississippi.

Farms of Catfish?

Some farms in Mississippi are different from most farms. They raise catfish! Of course, they are in water, but they are still called farms. There are more than 100 catfish farms in Mississippi. More than 64,000 acres of catfish ponds cover the state. In every acre, there are 6,000 catfish. The small town of Belzoni is known as the "Catfish Capital." It has a World Catfish Festival every spring.

FUN FACT More catfish are raised in the state of Mississippi than anywhere else in the United States.

North Carolina

North Carolina is a wide state. It stretches from the Atlantic Ocean in the east to the Great Smoky Mountains in the west. North Carolina also has a long string of islands that are east of its main shoreline. These sandy islands are called the Outer Banks. They can be reached by airplanes, ferryboats, and long bridges.

This bridge connects to Hatteras Island on North Carolina's Outer Banks.

Mystery of Roanoke Island

North Carolina has a mystery that has never been solved. The first English colony in America was settled on Roanoke Island in 1587. A few years later, the people mysteriously disappeared. It is thought that they may have left the island to live with the nearby Croatan Indians. No one knows for sure. No trace of these settlers was ever found, not even skeletons.

Virginia Dare was the first English child to be born in America. She was one of the Roanoke people who disappeared.

STATE FACTS

Statehood: November 21, 1789—12th state
Capital: Raleigh
Nickname: The Tar Heel State
Motto: To Be Rather Than to Seem
State Bird: Cardinal

State Flower: Dogwood
State Mammal: Gray squirrel
State Reptile: Eastern box turtle

What Is a Tar Heel?

People from North Carolina have an unusual nickname. They are called "Tar Heels." The nickname may have started during the Civil War. During a battle, soldiers from another Confederate state left the North Carolina soldiers to fight for themselves. The North Carolina soldiers were upset. They threatened to put tar on the other soldier's heels so they would "stick better" in future battles. General Robert E. Lee heard the story and liked it. He called the North Carolina soldiers the "Tar Heel Boys."

Let's Fly!

On December 17, 1903, the Wright brothers tested their flying machine on the Outer Banks near Kitty Hawk. They knew this spot had lots of wind, and they needed wind to get their airplane off the ground. Orville Wright was the first one to fly the plane off the ground for 12 seconds. He flew as far as half a football field. The brothers had three other short flights that day.

DID YOU KNOW?

North Carolina was the first state in the country to build a state museum of art.

Graveyard of the Atlantic

North Carolina has a long coastline. The coast is lovely, but it can be deadly too. Along the coast is a chain of sandy reefs and islands called the Outer Banks. These reefs and islands are dangerous because their locations change over time. The seas around them are often rough, and the currents are strong. More than 2,000 ships have wrecked along the Outer Banks. That's why this place is nicknamed "Graveyard of the Atlantic."

Land of Variety

North Carolina has three different areas of land. The land near the Atlantic Ocean is full of swamps and fertile farms. Farmers grow tobacco, soybeans, and cotton here. Most Carolinians live and work in the middle of the state. It is the busy heart of the state. This is where Raleigh, the state capital, and Charlotte, the largest city in the state, are located. The rugged Blue Ridge Mountains and the Smoky Mountains cover the western part of North Carolina. The tallest mountain is Mount Mitchell. It is 6,684 feet high.

South Carolina

South Carolina is shaped like a triangle. The Blue Ridge Mountains and the rolling hills of Piedmont are in the Up Country. Flat, sandy plains and swamps along the coast make up the Low Country. Columbia, the capital, sits in the middle. In 1670, the English built the city of Charleston. More than four million people live in South Carolina today. Companies in South Carolina make textiles, clothing, and chemical products. Fishers make a living by catching shrimp and crab.

STATE FACTS

Statehood: May 23, 1788—8th state
Capital: Columbia
Motto: While I Breathe, I Hope.
Nickname: The Palmetto State
State Bird: Carolina wren

State Flower: Carolina yellow Jessamine
State Tree: Palmetto tree
State Dog: Boykin spaniel
State Reptile: Loggerhead turtle
State Marine Animal: Bottlenose dolphin

Oh, Carolina!

In 1526, the Spanish settled near Winyah Bay along the coast of South Carolina. This was one of the first European settlements in the United States, but it did not last. When British colonists settled in this area, they named it "Carolina" in honor of England's King Charles I. In 1730, Carolina split into two separate colonies, North and South Carolina.

First Shot of the Civil War

South Carolina may be a small state, but it had a big part in the Civil War. It was the first state to leave the Union in 1860. This started the Civil War. Since the 1600s, South Carolina plantation owners have grown rice, cotton, and indigo (a flower that makes blue dye) in their fields. They used slaves from Africa to do the work. By the mid-1800s, some of the United States wanted to end slavery. The people of South Carolina did not agree with this. In 1861, South Carolina soldiers attacked Union soldiers at Fort Sumter in the Charleston Harbor. These were the first shots fired in the Civil War.

Go Gullah

Gullah is the name of a language and way of life for people who live on the islands off the South Carolina and Georgia coasts. Many of their ancestors were African slaves brought to the islands. The Gullah way of life and music survive to this day. Gullah is a mix of English and African languages. You may already know some Gullah words. The food names "yam" and "gumbo" both come from the Gullah language.

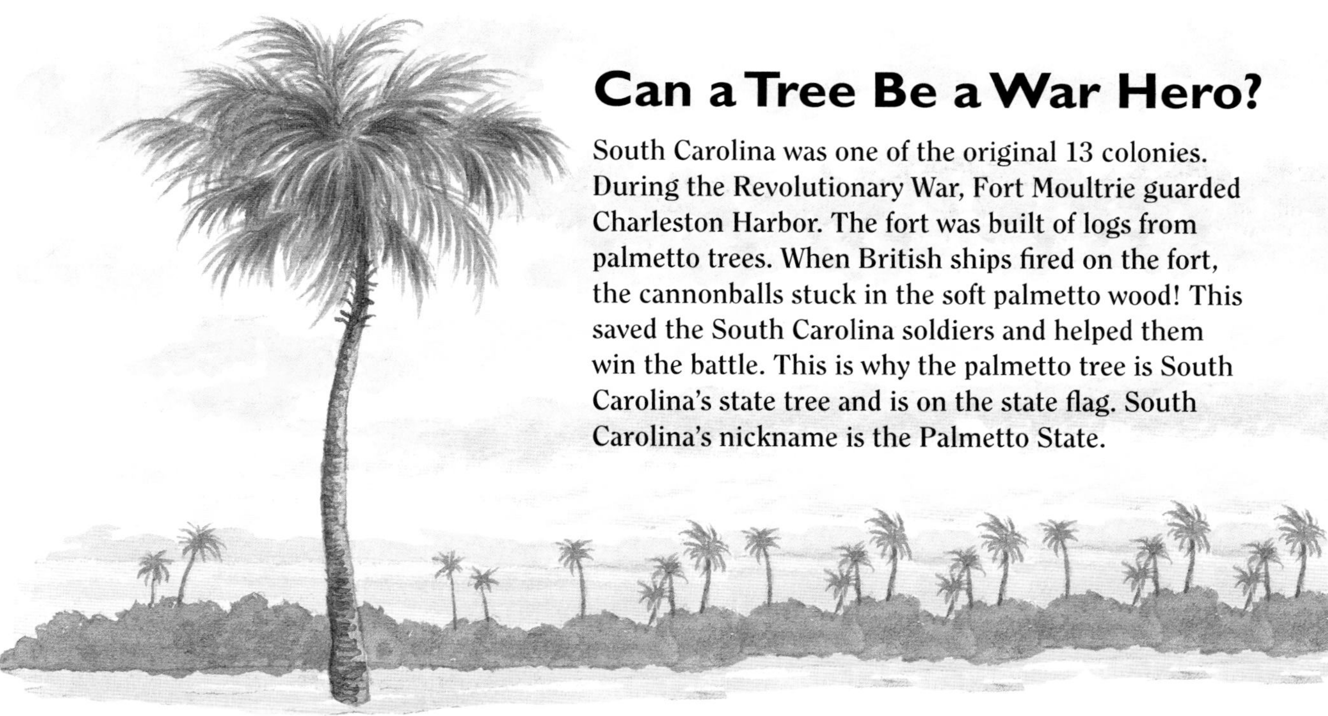

Can a Tree Be a War Hero?

South Carolina was one of the original 13 colonies. During the Revolutionary War, Fort Moultrie guarded Charleston Harbor. The fort was built of logs from palmetto trees. When British ships fired on the fort, the cannonballs stuck in the soft palmetto wood! This saved the South Carolina soldiers and helped them win the battle. This is why the palmetto tree is South Carolina's state tree and is on the state flag. South Carolina's nickname is the Palmetto State.

Let's Go to the Beach!

South Carolina has 187 miles of beautiful beaches and coastline. Visitors often go to famous beach towns such as Myrtle Beach and Hilton Head Island. Many families also enjoy going to smaller places. The Edisto Beach State Park has a dense forest, a salt marsh, and a 1.5-mile beach. This beach has many kinds of seashells and some of the tallest palmettos in the state. Huntington Beach State Park is known as one of the best bird-watching areas on the East Coast.

DID YOU KNOW?

South Carolina's state bird is the Carolina wren. When this bird sings, it sounds as if it is saying, "tea-ket-tle, tea-ket-tle."

FUN FACT The city of Myrtle Beach is in the middle of the Grand Strand, a 60-mile beach on the South Carolina coast. In the last 25 years, Myrtle Beach has become the most popular resort vacation spot on the East Coast.

Tennessee

The Great Smoky Mountains are in eastern Tennessee. The flat cotton-growing plains are in western Tennessee. In the middle of the state are rolling hills of bluegrass. This land is just right for raising horses, dairy cattle, beef cattle, and mules. Most people live in or near the cities of Memphis, Nashville, Knoxville, and Chattanooga. Some people work in factories making chemicals, electrical machinery, metals, and textiles.

STATE FACTS

Statehood: June 1, 1796—16th state
Capital: Nashville
Nickname: The Volunteer State
Motto: Agriculture and Commerce
State Bird: Mockingbird

State Flower: Iris
State Horse: Tennessee walking horse
State Wild Animal: Raccoon
State Tree: Tulip poplar

Trail of Tears

One of the saddest parts of Tennessee history is the "Trail of Tears." In the fall of 1838, the United States government forced 16,000 Cherokee people to leave their homelands in eastern Tennessee, northern Georgia, North Carolina, and Alabama. This was done to allow white settlers to move in and grow cotton on the land. The Cherokee people were gathered in Red Clay, Tennessee. Union soldiers, as many as 7,000, forced the Cherokee to walk across the state to the Indian Territory (what is now Oklahoma). Up to 4,000 Cherokee people died along the way. Many other Native Americans were also forced to leave their lands in the Southeast.

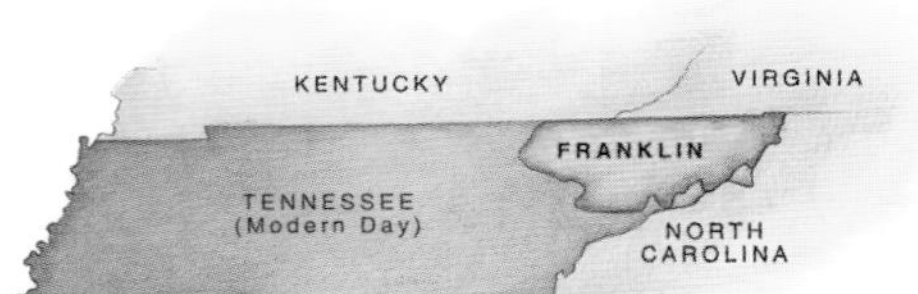

The State That Disappeared

Did you know that the United States almost had another state? In 1784, the people called it Frankland. It had been part of North Carolina. Settlers wrote a Constitution (a set of laws). They also elected a governor. But Frankland did not get enough votes from the United States Congress to become a state. They then changed the state's name to Franklin, hoping to get Benjamin Franklin's support, but that didn't work either. By 1789, North Carolina took back Franklin. In 1796, the land was turned over to the new state of Tennessee.

Cherokee Alphabet

Sequoyah was a Cherokee Indian who was born in eastern Tennessee, near Tuskeegee. He created an alphabet with 85 different symbols for the Cherokee people. Each symbol had a sound. He made a game of the alphabet and taught his young daughter Ayoka how to use it. In 1821, he and his daughter taught the written language to the Cherokee people. He also created a Cherokee newspaper.

DID YOU KNOW?

The Lost Sea in Sweetwater, Tennessee, is the largest underground lake in the United States.

Smoking Mountains?

The Great Smoky Mountains are between Tennessee and North Carolina. They are called the Great Smokies because of the fog that hangs over the mountain peaks. This makes them look mysterious, especially at sunrise or after a rain. The Great Smoky Mountains National Park is a protected park. It is often called "Wildflower National Park." There are 800 miles of hiking trails in this park. You can find plants in bloom here throughout the year. More than 1,000 bears live in these mountains.

FUN FACT More than 9 million people visit the Great Smoky Mountains National Park every year. This makes the Great Smokies the most visited national park in the country.

Tale of Two Tennessee Cities

Memphis and Nashville are two of Tennessee's biggest cities. Here's how they match up:

Memphis	Nashville
Largest Tennessee city	Second largest Tennessee city
Population: Approx. 670,000	Population: Approx. 636,000
Located in southwest Tennessee	Located in northcentral Tennessee
Home of Elvis Presley	Home of Country Music Hall of Fame
Location of Graceland	Location of Grand Ol' Opry
The Mississippi River runs through it	The Cumberland River runs through it

Virginia

Virginia is made up of three different regions. The eastern part is called the Tidewater. It has beaches, bays, and marshes. The central part of Virginia is the Piedmont. This word means "foot of the mountains." The Blue Ridge and Allegheny Mountains are in the western part of the state. The wide Shenandoah Valley runs between the mountain ridges.

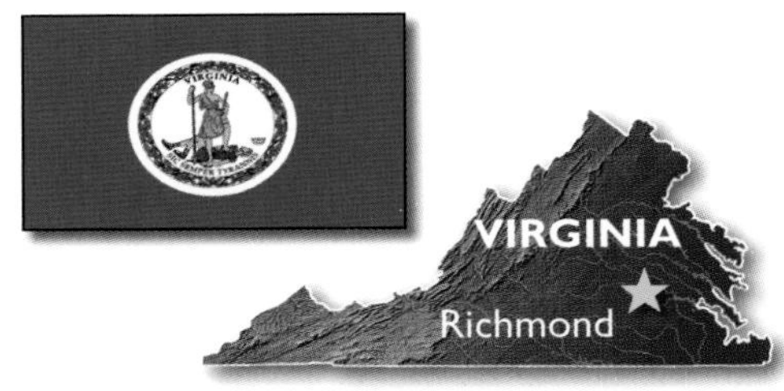

STATE FACTS

Statehood: June 25, 1788—10th state
Capital: Richmond
Nickname: Old Dominion or Mother of Presidents
Motto: Thus Always to Tyrants
State Bird: Cardinal

State Flower: American dogwood
State Dog: American foxhound
State Shell: Oyster shell
State Bat: Virginia big-eared bat
State Insect: Yellow swallowtail butterfly

Story of Pocahontas

Pocahontas was the daughter of a powerful Algonquin Indian chief named Powhatan. This Algonquin chief captured John Smith, the English leader of Jamestown. When Powhatan went to kill John Smith, Pocahontas threw herself on Smith and saved his life. The two became friends. Smith taught Pocahontas English, and she helped him learn Algonquin. This brought peace between the Algonquin nation and the English settlers. Several years later, she married a colonist named John Rolfe.

DID YOU KNOW?

***Misty of Chincoteague*, by Marguerite Henry, is a children's book. It is based on a story about a real pony from Chincoteague, Virginia.**

Growth of a Nation

Virginia has a rich history. This state is often called the "Birthplace of the Nation." As the United States grew, Virginia was always at the heart of the action.

1607
First English settlement in North America is founded in Jamestown.

1619
First slaves from Africa are brought to Jamestown.

1699
Williamsburg becomes the colony capital.

1780
The colony's capital moves to Richmond.

1781
The Revolutionary War ends. British General Cornwallis surrenders to General George Washington at Yorktown.

1861
Virginia breaks away from the Union. The first major battle of the Civil War is fought at Manassas.

1865
The Civil War ends when the South surrenders to the North at Appomattox.

Mother Virginia

Virginia is called the "Mother of Presidents." Eight United States presidents were born in Virginia: George Washington, Thomas Jefferson, James Madison, James Monroe, William Henry Harrison, John Tyler, Zachary Taylor, and Woodrow Wilson. Many of their homes still stand today. Visitors come from all across the country to see the homes of these American presidents. George Washington's home is in Mount Vernon. Thomas Jefferson's home of Monticello is near Charlottesville. James and Dolley Madison's home of Montpelier is near the town of Orange.

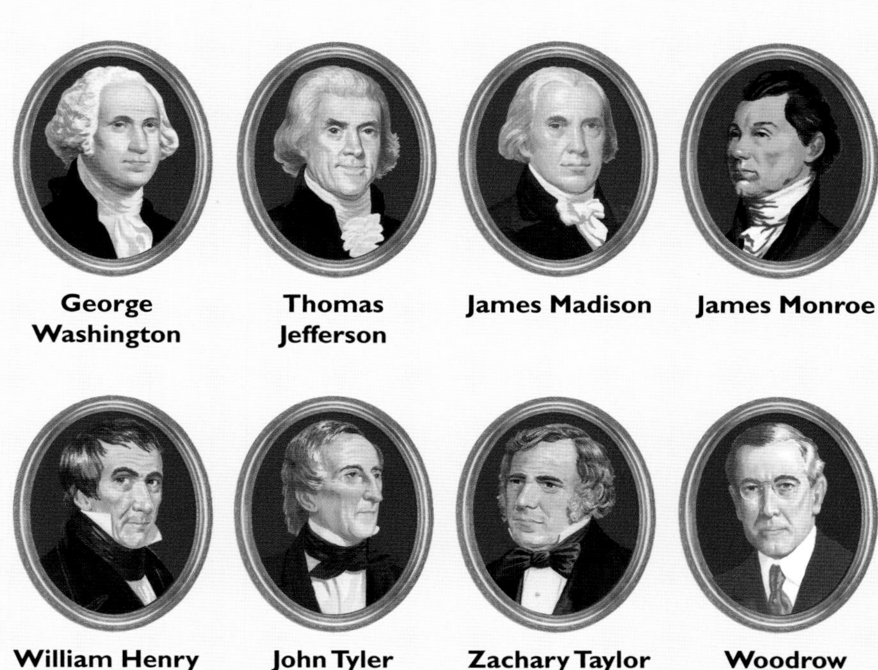

Ponies for Sale

Wild ponies live on Assateague Island in eastern Virginia. Every July, these ponies are driven across a narrow channel of water to the island of Chincoteague. The next day, about 80 of the young horses are sold at an auction. The money from the auction is used to take care of the remaining ponies in the herd. People believe that ponies have been living on Assateague Island for about 400 years.

FUN FACT Some people believe the ponies swam to Assateague's shores when a Spanish galleon ship carrying a cargo of horses sank off the Virginia coast in the 1600s.

Protecting Our Country

Many people in Virginia work to protect the United States. These people work for our government or military. The Department of Defense is in the Pentagon building in Arlington, Virginia. This is in northern Virginia near Washington, D.C. The southeastern part of Virginia near Norfolk has many important military bases. Many of the people who live here serve in the United States Army, Air Force, Navy, and Coast Guard.

West Virginia

West Virginia is called the Mountain State. The entire state is in the Appalachian Mountains. The state is full of valleys, rivers, forests, mountains, and deep gorges. About 1.8 million people live in West Virginia. Most of them live in small towns or rural areas. The largest city is Charleston. This is the capital of the state.

STATE FACTS

Statehood: June 20, 1863—35th state
Capital: Charleston
Nickname: The Mountain State
Motto: Mountaineers Are Always Free
State Bird: Cardinal

State Flower: Rhododendron
State Animal: Black bear
State Fish: Brook trout

Breaking Away

The people of West Virginia can be proud of their history. At the beginning of the Civil War, Virginia was a large state that controlled all the land that stretched far into the Appalachian Mountains. This is the area that later became West Virginia. The people in the eastern part of Virginia were in favor of slavery. But many people in the western part of Virginia wanted to end slavery. During the Civil War, the people from western Virginia decided to make a change. On June 20, 1863, they broke away from Virginia and formed their own state. They named it West Virginia.

Against Slavery

John Brown was an abolitionist (someone who fought to end slavery). In 1859, he and his followers raided Harpers Ferry. They captured the weapons of the United States Army in West Virginia. He hoped this would start a slave revolt, but it did not happen. Brown was captured and found guilty of revolt against his own country.

A Day for Mothers

Mother's Day began in West Virginia. When Anna M. Jarvis's mother died, she had an idea. One day each year should be set aside to honor mothers. She chose the second Sunday in May. In 1908, she held the first Mother's Day service at her church in Grafton, West Virginia. In 1914, President Woodrow Wilson made Mother's Day a national holiday. Today, you can visit the International Mother's Day Shrine and Museum in the town of Grafton.

Let's Go Rafting!

It takes courage to go white-water rafting. People who like this thrill enjoy the rivers in West Virginia. The Gauley River National Recreation Area has 25 miles of fast-moving water. The Gauley River also has more than 100 rapids. The names of these rapids are fun and exciting, including Lost Paddle, Pillow Rock, and Heaven Help Us.

FUN FACT The New River Gorge Bridge in West Virginia is the longest steel-arch bridge in the United States. It spans 1,815 feet across the New River Canyon.

Coal Mining and the Future

Coal is mined from the ground and used to make energy. Coal mining is hard and dangerous work. There is always a risk of an explosion or a mine collapse. People of West Virginia have been mining coal for more than 100 years. West Virginia is one of the nation's leaders in coal. But the need for coal is changing. Oil, gas, and other kinds of energy are slowly replacing coal. West Virginians are finding other ways to make a living. Tourism is one business that is growing in the state. West Virginians run motels and restaurants for people who visit their beautiful state.

DID YOU KNOW?

To build the Charleston airport in West Virginia, workers chopped off the top of mountains and filled in the surrounding valleys with tons of dirt.

Southwest

The Southwest is known for its deserts, mountains, canyons, and wide-open spaces. This area is often hot and dry. It is the driest part of the country because of its major deserts. Temperatures in the summer often reach well over 100 degrees. In the mountains, the temperatures are cooler. During winter, snow falls on the high peaks. People have lived in the Southwest for thousands of years.

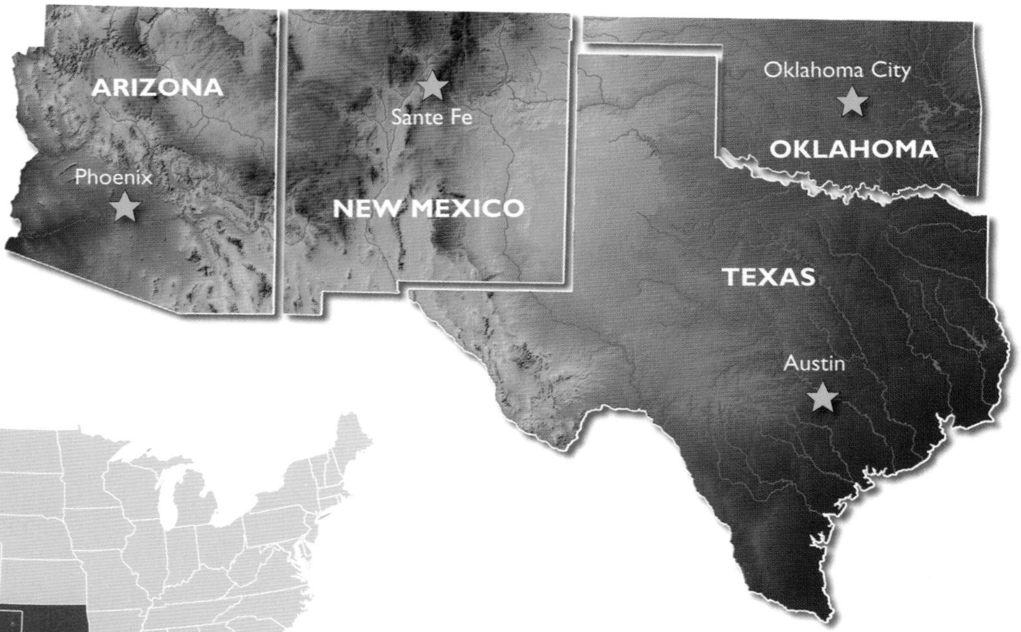

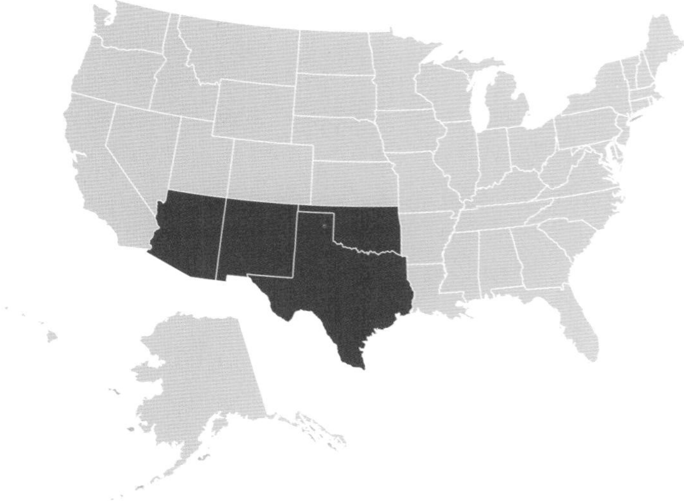

Arizona

New Mexico

Oklahoma

Texas

Who Lived Here First?

The Southwest region has not always belonged to the United States. Native Americans lived in this area first. In the 1500s, explorers from Spain took the land. By 1821, Mexico had control of the Southwest. But the United States also wanted the land. Texas separated from Mexico in 1836 to become its own country. Later, it joined the United States. The United States claimed most of New Mexico and Arizona after a war with Mexico in the 1840s. The oldest settlement in the Southwest is Oraibi, a Hopi village in northeast Arizona. People have lived in this settlement since about 1100.

A Sight to Behold

The Southwest is full of colorful beauty. In Texas and Oklahoma, there are flat lands and rocky hills. In New Mexico and Arizona, rugged mountains and wide deserts cover the land. Monument Valley runs through Utah and Arizona, while the Grand Canyon is in Arizona. The size and colors of the red sandstones are breathtaking. A Spanish explorer named the Painted Desert in Arizona. He called it "El Desierto Pintado." He thought it looked like the colors of the sunset.

A Great Place to Live

Native Americans have lived in the Southwest for thousands of years. They built villages called pueblos. Pueblos are flat-roofed stone houses, often made against cliff walls. The Navajo, Apache, and Hopi Indians call the Southwest their home. But people in the Southwest come from many backgrounds. Many are Hispanic Americans. Some people who live here came from Europe. The number of people living in the Southwest today is growing. Phoenix and Dallas are among the fastest growing cities in the country. Arizona and Texas are among the fastest growing states. Many people like the warm, dry weather here.

Above and Below the Land

The land in the Southwest may look dry. But where there is enough water, farmers grow cotton and other crops. Ranchers raise beef cattle and sheep. The land also has many things below the ground that people need. Natural gas, oil, copper—and even gold and silver—are mined from the land.

Arizona

Arizona has wide deserts, red cliffs, high mountains—and pine forests too. It is a land of warm beauty. Dams were built to give the state a steady supply of water. Farmers water their fields. Ranchers herd their cattle. More than a hundred years ago, miners found gold, silver, and copper. Mining towns were built. Back then, they were often wild, lawless places. For a long time, people thought of Arizona as the Wild West.

STATE FACTS

Statehood: February 14, 1912—48th state
Capital: Phoenix
Nickname: The Grand Canyon State
Motto: God Enriches
State Bird: Cactus wren

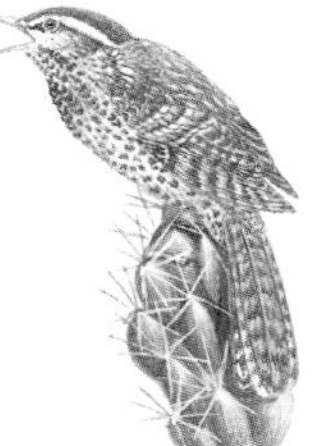

State Flower: Saguaro cactus blossom
State Tree: Palo verde
State Reptile: Arizona ridge-nosed rattlesnake

A Painted Desert?

There is a desert in Arizona that has many miles of blue, yellow, red, pink, and tan sands and rocks. Navajo Indians used these colorful sands to make sand paintings. The area is called the "Painted Desert." It is part of the Petrified Forest National Park. This park has many ancient logs that have turned to stone.

Arizona's First People

Native Americans were the first people to live in Arizona. They lived on the land for over a thousand years. The Spanish came north from Mexico in 1539 looking for gold. Arizona became part of Mexico. In the mid-1800s, the United States fought Mexico to take control of Arizona. At the same time, Native Americans fought to keep their lands. By 1886, the last of the Native Americans surrendered to the United States. They were then placed on reservations in the state, which cover almost one-fourth of the land. More than 320,000 Native Americans live in Arizona today—they are free to live anywhere.

This Canyon Is Grand!

The Grand Canyon is called grand for a reason. It is a mile deep and 277 river miles long. In some places, the Grand Canyon is 18 miles wide. It is in northwestern Arizona. It was formed by the Colorado River. There are many rock layers in the Grand Canyon. It took millions of years for the river to work its way down through those layers. Rain, snow, and streams—which can wear away rock—carved out the sides of the Grand Canyon.

FUN FACT More than five million people visit the Grand Canyon each year. Most people stay near the rim of the canyon. Others hike all the way to the bottom.

Night Skies

What do Pluto and Arizona have in common? An astronomer at the Lowell Observatory in Flagstaff, Arizona, was the first person to see Pluto. His name was Clyde Tombaugh. The year was 1930. He was just 24 years old. The Lowell Observatory is still used today for research. If you like looking at the stars, you can go to the Lowell Observatory and look through the large telescopes. You can even climb the spiral staircase to see the telescope that Clyde Tombaugh used to discover Pluto.

DID YOU KNOW?

Arizona did not become a state until 1912 because people thought of the area as part of the Wild West.

Prickly Facts

The saguaro cactus blossom is Arizona's state flower. It grows in the Sonoran Desert. This desert is in the southwestern part of the state. The saguaro cactus can grow to be 50 feet tall. It grows slowly. It may grow one inch in its first eight years. Then it may take 50 to 75 years to grow its first arm. It first blooms when the cactus is 50 to 75 years old. It is considered an adult when it is 125 years old!

New Mexico

New Mexico has rugged mountains, wide deserts, lush grasslands, deep gorges, and huge caves. The Rocky Mountains run down the middle of the northern area, while deserts take up the southern part of the state. It may have the word Mexico in its name, but it is not part of Mexico. It is part of the United States. More than two million people live here. The biggest cities are Albuquerque and Las Cruces. There are many science labs and military bases in New Mexico.

STATE FACTS

Statehood: January 6, 1912—47th state
Capital: Santa Fe
Nickname: Land of Enchantment
Motto: It Grows As It Goes
State Bird: Greater roadrunner

State Flower: Yucca
State Tree: Piñon pine
State Gem: Turquoise
State Insect: Tarantula hawk wasp
State Cookie: Bizcochito

New Mexico, Old History

Native Americans have lived in New Mexico for at least 10,000 years. These groups include the Mogollon, Anasazi, Pueblo, Navajo, and Apache Indians. In the mid-1500s, Spanish explorers came to this land and took it over for Spain. From 1810 to 1821, Mexico fought against Spain, and this land became part of Mexico.

American traders and settlers started coming to this area. After a war with Mexico, the United States took control of New Mexico. It became a United States territory in 1848. But it did not become a state until 1912. Today, New Mexico is home to three major groups of people: Native Americans, Hispanic Americans, and European Americans.

DID YOU KNOW?

Truth or Consequences is a city in New Mexico. It is named after a 1940s radio quiz show.

Living on the Edge

The Anasazi Indians last lived in New Mexico about 700 years ago. They built their villages out of stone, plaster, and sun-dried bricks. Some buildings were five stories tall and had many rooms. Other buildings were made against sides of cliffs. Still others were built on top of flat-topped hills.

FUN FACT The Anasazi Indians used wooden ladders to climb to their homes. Ruins of these villages are still in northern New Mexico.

Underground Surprise

In 1898, a 16-year-old cowboy named Jim White found the Carlsbad Caverns by accident. He spotted the caverns when he saw thousands of bats coming out of a hole in the ground. The Carlsbad Caverns are a set of 117 giant caves. They are in southern New Mexico. One room is called "The Big Room." It is 2,000 feet long and about 200 feet high. That's big enough to hold many sports stadiums. And the bats are still there—more than 300,000 of them!

An international festival of hot air balloons is held every year in Albuquerque.

A Bear-able Cause

In the 1940s, the Forest Service had started a program to teach kids how to prevent fires that starred a character named Smokey Bear: "Remember...Only YOU Can Prevent Wildfires!" A real-life black bear cub was found after a New Mexico forest fire in 1950. It was found burned and clinging to the branch of a scorched pine tree. The cute little bear won the hearts of the American people. The fire prevention program became a huge success.

Meeting Place for States

Do you think you can be in four places at once? Well, at the Four Corners Monument you can! The Four Corners Monument is the only place in the United States where four states meet in one place. The northwest corner of New Mexico meets the corners of Arizona, Utah, and Colorado. You can go to the monument and put a hand and foot in each state!

Oklahoma

The name Oklahoma comes from the Choctaw Indian words *okla humma*, which mean "red people." In the 1800s, this land belonged to Native Americans. Today, farmers in Oklahoma grow wheat and raise cattle. The state is rich in natural gas and oil. Many people in Oklahoma work in factories repairing airplanes. About 3.7 million people live in Oklahoma. Many of them live in the cities of Tulsa and Oklahoma City.

STATE FACTS

Statehood: November 16, 1907—46th state
Capital: Oklahoma City
Nickname: The Sooner State
Motto: Labor Conquers All Things
State Bird: Scissor-tailed flycatcher

State Flower: Oklahoma rose
State Amphibian: Bullfrog
State Tree: Redbud

A Native American family outside their hut in Indian Territory in 1900

Indian Territory

In the early 1800s, settlers in the eastern United States wanted more space. The government made the Choctaw, Cherokee, Creek, Chickasaw, and Seminole Indians give up their land. They moved west to what was called "Indian Territory" (now Oklahoma). Many Native Americans died along the way. This sad journey was called the "Trail of Tears."

No settlers were allowed on this land for many years. But in 1889, this rule changed. The government took more land away from the Native Americans and gave it to the settlers. Oklahoma became a state in 1907. About 295,000 Native Americans live in Oklahoma today. It is the center for 39 Indian nations. More Native Americans live in Oklahoma than in any other state.

What Is a Sooner?

In 1889, the United States government allowed settlers to own land in Indian Territory. But there was a rule: No one could enter until April 22. About 50,000 settlers lined up at the border. At noon, a pistol was fired. The settlers charged ahead to claim the land. Some were on horses and wagons. Others were on foot. But some people snuck onto the land ahead of this time. They were nicknamed "Sooners."

Here is a view from Mount Scott in the Wichita Mountains wildlife refuge.

Oklahoma Mountains

Much of Oklahoma is farmland or rangeland. But Oklahoma also has four small mountain ranges. The Ozark and Ouachita Mountains are covered with trees. They are in the far eastern part of the state. The Arbuckle Mountains are in the south. The Wichita Mountains are a rocky range in the southwestern corner of the state. All these mountain ranges offer people the chance to hike.

The Arbuckle Mountains have trails for dirt-biking!

The Five Moons

In 1967, five Native Americans became famous ballerinas. They were known as the "Five Moons." Their names are Yvonne Chouteau, Marjorie and Maria Tallchief, Rosella Hightower, and Moscelyne Larkin. There is a series of bronze sculptures in Tulsa, Oklahoma, in honor of these five ballerinas.

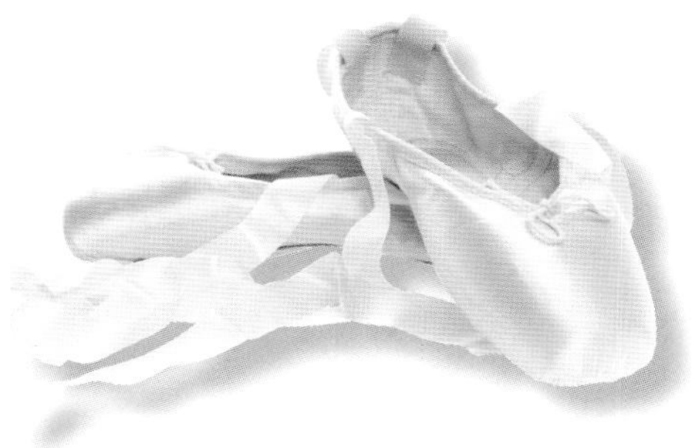

Famous Folksinger

Woody Guthrie was an American folksinger. He grew up in Okemah, Oklahoma. When he was a teenager, he traveled across the country playing his guitar and singing. He wrote nearly 3,000 songs, mostly about hard times and ordinary people.

His most popular song is "This Land Is Your Land":

This land is your land,

This land is my land,

From California to the New York island,

From the redwood forest to the Gulf Stream waters,

This land was made for you and me.

DID YOU KNOW?

The National Cowboy Hall of Fame is in Oklahoma City.

The *Coming Through the Rye* sculpture by Frederic Remington at Oklahoma City's National Cowboy Hall of Fame

Texas

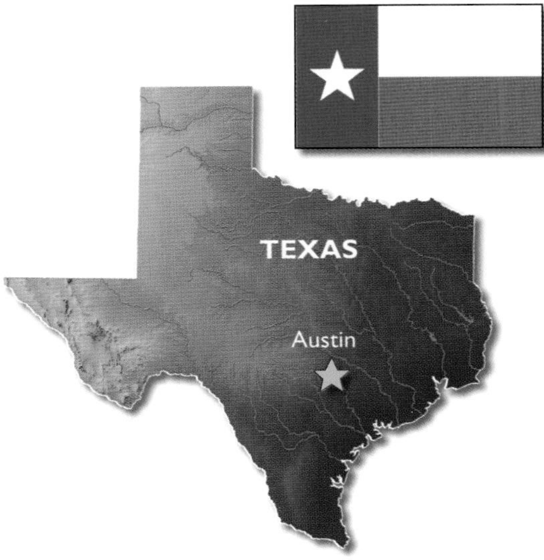

Long ago, the Caddo Indians lived in the land that is now Texas. Their word for friends sounded like "Tayshas." The Spanish explorers who came to Texas spelled the word as "Tejas." Later settlers changed Tejas to Texas. Almost 25 million people live in Texas today. It has more people than any other state except California. The major cities are Houston, Dallas, Austin, San Antonio, and El Paso.

The Father of Texas

Stephen F. Austin was born in Virginia in 1793. He helped bring 300 American families to Texas when it was not yet part of the United States. He set up the first American colony in Texas in 1822. He is known as "The Father of Texas." Austin, the capital of Texas, is named after him. A state university and college, as well as many smaller schools, are also named after him.

STATE FACTS

Statehood: December 29, 1845—28th state
Capital: Austin
Nickname: The Lone Star State
Motto: Friendship
State Bird: Mockingbird

State Flower: Bluebonnet
State Tree: Pecan
State Gem: Texas blue topaz
State Dish: Chili

Battle Cry of Texas

In the 1820s, Texas was part of Mexico. But American settlers wanted to be free of Mexico. War broke out in 1835. The Texans fought the Mexican Army at the Alamo, an old chapel and fort in San Antonio. The Mexican Army had surrounded about 142 Texas soldiers for 13 days. The Texans lost this battle. Six weeks later, the Texans fought the Mexican Army in San Jacinto. As they fought, they shouted the battle cry, "Remember the Alamo!" Texas won the battle and became a free land.

Six Flags Over Texas

Texas has belonged to six different countries. First, the countries of Spain, France, and Mexico claimed Texas as their own. In 1836, Texas became its own country. In 1845, Texas joined the United States. But that didn't last. During the Civil War (1861–1865), Texas broke away from the United States and joined the Confederacy. When the Civil War was over, Texas rejoined the United States.

Spain	1519–1685; 1690–1821
France	1685–1690
Mexico	1821–1836
Republic of Texas	1836–1845
Confederacy	1861–1865
United States	1845–1861; 1865–present

Six Flags over Texas is also the name of a giant amusement park. It is in Arlington, Texas.

A Blue Bonnet?

The bluebonnet is the state flower of Texas. They grow on the Texas prairies and along the Texas highways. They bloom from March until May. Bluebonnets have bright blue petals with white centers. The petals reminded the settlers of the bonnets (hats) that women wore to protect themselves from the hot Texas sun. So they named this flower bluebonnet.

Black Gold, Texas Tea

In 1901, Anthony Lucas was drilling at Spindletop Hill, Texas. Suddenly a gush of oil shot 150 feet into the air. It took nine days to cap (cover) the well. After that, oil was discovered in many other parts of Texas. More oil has been drilled from the ground in Texas than any other state. Oil is big business in Texas.

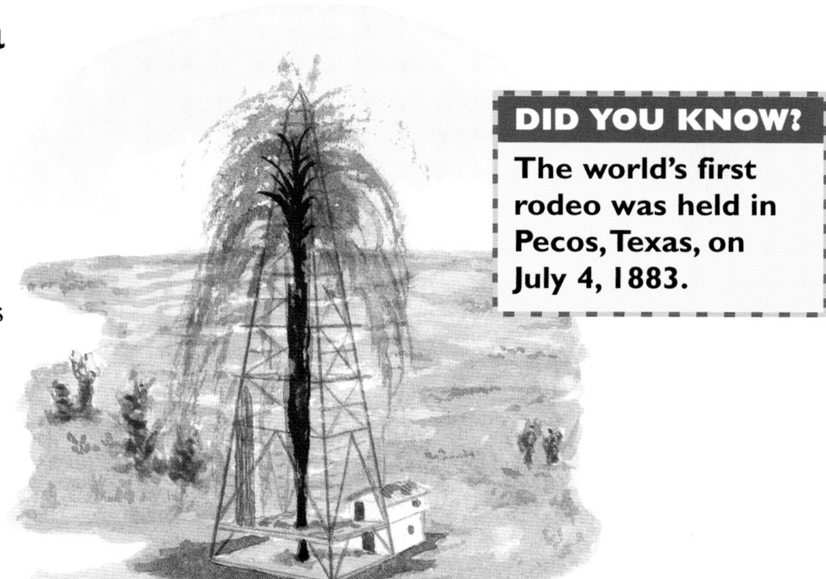

DID YOU KNOW?

The world's first rodeo was held in Pecos, Texas, on July 4, 1883.

Texas Presidents

Four United States presidents are from Texas. But only two of them were actually born in Texas.

Dwight D. Eisenhower
born in Denison, Texas. He was raised in Kansas.

Lyndon B. Johnson
born near Stonewall, Texas. He went to high school and college in Texas.

George H. W. Bush
born in Milton, Massachusetts. He moved to western Texas as an adult.

George W. Bush
born in New Haven, Connecticut. He grew up in Midland, Texas, and Houston, Texas.

Big State, Big Businesses

Texas is a big state. It is bigger than any other state in the United States except for Alaska. Texas is also a leader. It is first in the country in oil, cotton, cattle, and sheep. Texas also has other strong businesses. In eastern Texas, forests are used for timber. In Dallas and Fort Worth, computer equipment is made. In southeastern Texas, fishers catch shrimp and oysters.

DID YOU KNOW?

The King Ranch in Texas is bigger than the state of Rhode Island.

Texas Longhorns

In the late 1800s, Texas ranchers raised large herds of cattle on the Texas plains. But they had a problem. How would they sell the cattle to people in the east? The nearest railroad was more than 1,000 miles away. The solution: Cowboys "drove" large herds of cattle through Texas. They followed the Chisholm Trail north to Kansas.

FUN FACT The Texas Longhorns is also the name of the University of Texas sports teams.

Big State, Small Animals

Texas is a big state, but it is home to many small (and unusual) animals.

The **horned lizard** is covered with pointy spines. It defends itself by shooting blood from its eyes.

The **armadillo** is a mammal that has a leathery shell. The shell looks like a coat of armor.

The **prairie dog** lives in west Texas. Hundreds of them live in underground "towns" that are connected by tunnels.

The **roadrunner** can race 15 miles per hour.

The **cockroach** is a household pest. There's even a folk song about this insect. It's called "La Cucaracha."

Space Center

The Lyndon B. Johnson Space Center is in Houston, Texas. It is named after President Johnson, who was born in Texas. This is the headquarters for all piloted space flights from America. Astronauts train here for their missions. Houston's Mission Control experts guide and keep an eye on each spacecraft that blasts off from Cape Canaveral in Florida. They help the astronauts get their spacecraft back on earth safely.

Here is a look inside the cockpit of the Space Shuttle.

Strong Texas Women

Barbara Jordan became a United States Representative in 1973. She was the first African American from Texas in Congress. She grew up in Houston.

Ann Richards was the governor of Texas from 1991 to 1995. She was the second female governor of Texas. She grew up in Waco.

Nastia Liukin won a gold medal in the 2008 Summer Olympics. She was the all-around woman's champion in gymnastics. She grew up in Plano, Texas.

Mountain

The Rocky Mountains are the most spectacular mountains in the country. They run through every state in the Mountain region. The peaks are high. The slopes are steep. Rivers and streams flow through the valleys. These states also have wide plains and high rangeland, where ranchers raise beef cattle, sheep, and hay. Fewer people live in the Mountain region than in other parts of the United States. This region was one of the last areas of the country to be settled.

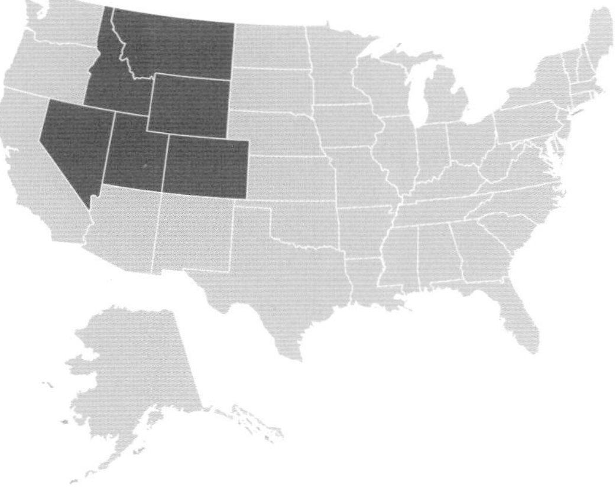

Colorado

Idaho

Montana

Nevada

Utah

Wyoming

Region of Wilderness

The Mountain region has 12 national parks. The parks are large and full of trees, lakes, animals, and hiking trails. Visitors come to see the beautiful scenery and wildlife. One of the most popular places is Yellowstone National Park. Three million people visit this park each year. National parks are not the only places to find great scenery. The Mountain region also has many national monuments, forests, and wilderness areas.

A herd of bison moves quickly along the Firehole River in Yellowstone National Park.

Chief Sevara, of the Ute nation, and his family lived in Colorado.

The First People

Native Americans have lived in the Mountain region for at least 12,000 years. When miners and settlers from the East came to this area, they forced the Native Americans off their lands. Today, many Native Americans still live in the mountain states. The Ute Indians live in Utah, New Mexico, and Colorado. Members of the Nez Percé live in Idaho. The Shoshone Indians live in all the mountain states. People from Crow and Assiniboine nations live in Montana.

What's Under the Ground?

Miners were the original settlers of many towns in the Mountain region. These miners came from the East looking for gold and silver. The people in Butte, Montana, ended up finding a different treasure. They found copper. Today, mining is still important to the region. Many resources other than gold and silver are mined from the ground. These resources are coal, oil, and natural gas.

Let It Snow

In the winter, it snows a lot on the mountains. This is good news for people who like to ski. Ski resorts in Colorado and Utah often get more than 400 inches of snow each year. That is more than 30 feet—about as tall as three basketball hoops stacked on top of each other! Snow makes it difficult to travel in the mountains. Sometimes, people put chains on the tires of their cars or trucks. This helps the tires grip the snow. Other roads are so dangerous during snowy conditions they are closed for the entire winter.

Colorado

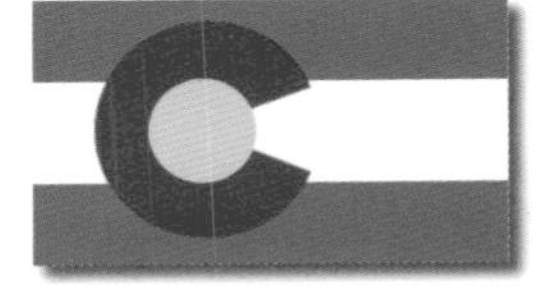

Colorado has tall mountains. More than 50 of them are taller than 14,000 feet. Colorado's highest peak is Mount Elbert. It is 14,433 feet tall. Visitors go to the mountains at all times of the year. In winter, millions of people ski and snowboard down the slopes. The eastern part of Colorado has no mountains. It is in the Great Plains. Ranchers use the land to raise beef cattle and sheep. In some places, farmers grow wheat, corn, and hay.

Colorado's Famous Mountain

Pikes Peak is one of Colorado's famous mountains. It is 14,115 feet tall. In 1806, Zebulon Pike saw the mountain when he was exploring the Louisiana Purchase. He was not able to climb it. In 1893, Katherine Lee Bates rode to the top of Pikes Peak in a carriage. The view inspired her to write a poem. It became the song "America the Beautiful." Today, people take a train or drive to the top of Pikes Peak on the Pikes Peak Highway. About a half-million people make it to the top of the mountain each year.

FUN FACT Every summer, there is a car race to the top of Pikes Peak. It starts at 9,390 feet above sea level, and it ends at 14,110 feet.

STATE FACTS:

Statehood: August 1, 1876—38th state
Capital: Denver
Nickname: The Centennial State
Motto: Nothing Without the Deity
State Bird: Lark bunting

State Flower: White and lavender columbine
State Tree: Colorado blue spruce
Animal: Rocky Mountain bighorn sheep
State Gemstone: Aquamarine
State Fish: Greenback cutthroat trout

DID YOU KNOW?

Explorers from Spain named Colorado. The name means, "colored red." This is because many of the cliffs and rocks of Colorado are red.

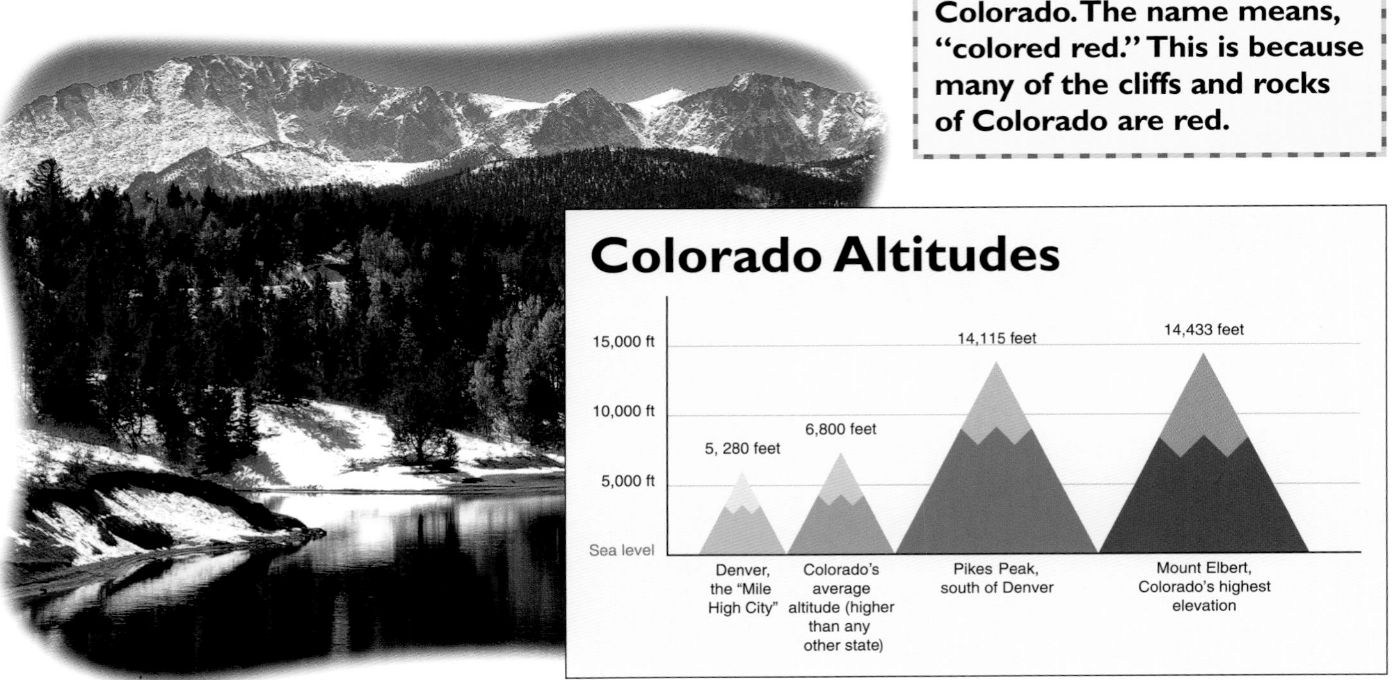

Cliff Life

In 1888, two cowboys made a discovery in southwest Colorado. They found a "Cliff Palace." This was the home of the Ancient Puebloans. About 800 years ago, the Pueblos had built villages under the overhang of a cliff. Some of the buildings were so big they had 150 rooms. Many also had a "kiva." This was an underground room for ceremonies. If you visit Mesa Verde National Park, you can walk near these ancient ruins.

What's Made at a Mint?

Mint isn't just a flavor. It's also a place where coins are made. The United States has a mint in Denver. Millions of pennies, nickels, dimes, quarters, and other coins are made here. If a coin has a tiny D on it, you know it was made at the United States Mint in Denver. Colorado's new state quarter shows the Great Sand Dunes National Monument. It will be released in 2014 and will be made in the Denver Mint.

Winter Fun

Where can you find winter fun in Colorado? Everywhere! Winter sports are very popular in Colorado. The state is known around the world for its great places to ski. People come from all over the world to ski and snowboard down many slopes.

Idaho

Idaho has steep mountains and thick forests. It is known as the land of potatoes! Idaho farmers grow one out of every three potatoes in the United States. They also grow wheat and sugar beets. Workers in Idaho make wood products, paper products, and computer parts. Many new jobs in Idaho have to do with science and technology. About 1.5 million people live in Idaho.

Idaho's many farms grow piles of potatoes.

STATE FACTS

Statehood: July 3, 1890—43rd state
Capital: Boise
Nickname: The Gem State
Motto: Let It Be Perpetual
State Bird: Mountain bluebird

State Flower: Syringa
State Horse: Appaloosa
State Fish: Cutthroat trout
State Fruit: Huckleberry
State Tree: Western white pine

Lava Land

About 2,000 years ago, hot lava flowed over southern Idaho. There are black lava beds at Craters of the Moon National Monument. The ground looks black and lifeless. But 280 kinds of animals and 660 different kinds of plants live there. If you visit, you can explore caves made by the lava tubes. One of them is called Boy Scout Cave. It was discovered by a group of Boy Scouts in 1927.

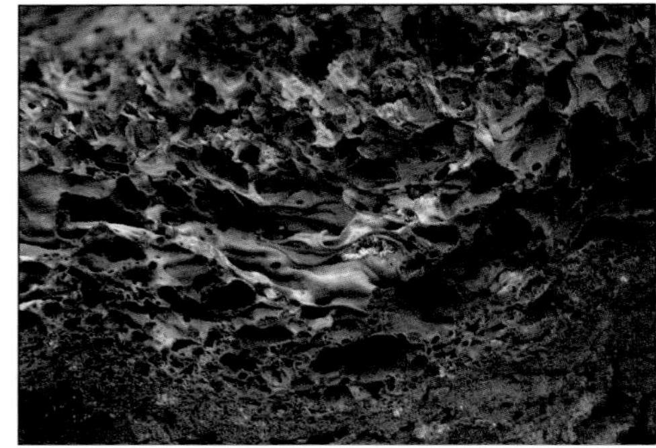

FUN FACT Scientists at the Idaho National Laboratory study nuclear energy (energy taken from atoms). The laboratory is near a tiny town called Atomic City.

Frozen Waterfall and River?

Idaho has hundreds of underground caverns. The most famous and spectacular cavern is Crystal Ice Cave near Pocatello. This ice cave has many interesting ice and stone formations. There is even a frozen waterfall and frozen river in this cavern!

The Nez Percé

For thousands of years, the Nez Percé have lived on the land that is now Idaho. In 1855, United States leaders promised the Nez Percé a large reserve of land for fishing and hunting. This promise was broken. In 1877, Chief Joseph tried to move 800 of his people to Canada where they could live freely. The United States soldiers chased them for more than 1,100 miles through Idaho, Wyoming, and Montana. The Nez Percé were captured 40 miles from Canada. There is a Nez Percé Historic Site near Lewiston, Idaho. If you visit, you can learn about Chief Joseph's trail.

DID YOU KNOW?

Philo Farnsworth from Beaver Creek, Idaho, was 15 years old when he invented the television.

This girl is taking part in a patato-picking contest in Idaho.

Idaho's Longest River

The Snake River is Idaho's longest river. It starts in Yellowstone National Park in Wyoming and flows through southern Idaho. Then it turns north. It flows through Hells Canyon, which is is almost 8,000 feet deep. That is almost a half-mile deeper than the Grand Canyon! It is the deepest river gorge in the United States. This area is famous for boating, fishing, and wildlife. Most of Idaho's larger cities are near the Snake River. They are Idaho Falls, Pocatello, and Boise.

Potato Party!

Idaho grows more than 13 billion potatoes each year. That's a lot of "spuds." The town of Shelley, Idaho, celebrates Spud Day. Every September, the town has a parade and a potato-picking contest. There's also a tug of war over a pit of mashed potatoes. The mashed potatoes are made in a cement mixer. For fun, you can try this: Look at the potatoes in the grocery store. If the potato bag has an outline of Idaho, you know where the potatoes were grown!

Montana

The name Montana comes from a Spanish word that means "mountain." The Rocky Mountains tower above the western part of Montana. This state is also called "Big Sky Country." The plains cover the eastern part of the state. The sky looks extra large over this area. Montana is the fourth largest state. Farmers here raise beef cattle and grow wheat, and miners remove oil, natural gas, and coal from the ground. Montana's biggest cities are Billings and Missoula.

Battle of the Little Bighorn

Native Americans fought a losing war to save their way of life in Montana. But on June 25, 1876, Lakota Indian warrior Crazy Horse led an army of Sioux and Cheyenne Indians against the United States Army. He defeated George A. Custer and his troops at the Battle of the Little Bighorn.

STATE FACTS

Statehood: November 8, 1889—41st state
Capital: Helena
Nickname: The Treasure State
Motto: Oro y Plata (Gold and Silver)
State Bird: Western meadowlark

State Flower: Bitterroot
State Animal: Grizzly bear
State Fossil: *Maiasaura* (Duck-billed dinosaur)
State Tree: Ponderosa pine

The Wild Life

Montana's wildlife is really wild!

The **grizzly bear** has claws that are four inches long.

The **porcupine** has 30,000 quills. Babies are born with quills that harden in an hour.

The **mountain lion** is found in the mountains, foothills, and plains.

The **male bighorn** sheep battles other males by crashing horns together.

The average **elk** can weigh 1,000 pounds. It is also called a wapiti.

The **trumpeter swan** has a wingspan of nearly seven feet.

More grizzly bears are found in Montana than anywhere else in the lower 48 states.

Beautiful Stones

A sapphire is a beautiful gem. Most sapphires are clear blue. Many have been found in central Montana near rivers and creeks. The most valuable sapphires were found in a place called Yogo Gulch. Some of them are worth more than diamonds. No wonder Montana is nicknamed the Treasure State. Some of Montana's sapphires are on display at the Smithsonian Museum in Washington, D.C.

DID YOU KNOW?

Tyrannosaurus rex **and** ***Triceratops*** **fossils were found in northeastern Montana near the town of Jordan.**

Shining Mountains

Glacier National Park is in northern Montana. It has mountains, forests, and deep blue lakes. It also has more than 1,000 kinds of wildflowers. Glacier National Park has 25 glaciers. They are made of hard-packed ice and snow. The glaciers have shaped the mountains and the valleys with their movement. Native Americans called this area the "Shining Mountains."

Camping and fishing are popular activities in Bozeman.

Who Comes to Montana?

Native Americans were the first people to live on the plains and mountains of Montana. In the early 1800s, Lewis and Clark explored the land. Fur traders and missionaries came next. In the 1860s, miners found gold at Grasshopper Creek. People rushed to Montana. Later, copper was found near Butte, Montana. It was worth billions of dollars. Butte was called "the richest hill on earth." Today, visitors come to Montana to fish, hunt, hike, and camp.

Nevada

Most of Nevada is in the Great Basin, a huge desert that covers parts of six states. Nevada has the least amount of rainfall of any state. It is covered with quiet mountains and dry valleys. Sagebrush and cacti grow on the dry land. Ranchers raise beef cattle, and sheep, and grow hay. There are many towns in Nevada that remind people of the Old West. Las Vegas and Reno are two of Nevada's big cities that attract many visitors.

STATE FACTS

Statehood: Oct. 31, 1864—36th state
Capital: Carson City
Nickname: The Silver State
Motto: All for Our Country
State Bird: Mountain bluebird
State Flower: Sagebrush
State Animal: Desert bighorn sheep
State Metal: Silver
State Reptile: Desert tortoise
State Grass: Indian ricegrass
State Tree: Single-leaf piñon and Bristlecone pine

Valley of Fire State Park

DID YOU KNOW?

Nevada is mostly desert, but the Sierra Nevada and Ruby Mountains have snow for half the year.

Silver and Gold!

In the mid-1800s, people found gold on Mount Davidson. But there was a problem. Blue-gray mud stuck to the miners' shovels. It was not a problem for long. The blue-gray mud turned out to be silver! Thousands of people moved to Nevada and built mining towns such as Virginia City. It was called "the richest town on earth." By 1877, millions of dollars of gold and silver had been mined. But the supply of gold and silver did not last. The price of silver fell, and the people left town. Many mining towns turned into ghost towns. People can still visit the old Nevada mining towns and see the historic buildings of the Wild West.

Virginia City still has many historic buildings.

Visit Nevada

Much of Nevada's land is dry and not good for farming. So people in Nevada make money from the millions of visitors who vacation there every year. Visitors enjoy the bright cities of Las Vegas and Reno. They visit the gambling casinos. They go to shows to see famous performers. They stay in large and fancy hotels.

Many people also visit Lake Tahoe in the Sierra Nevada Mountains. In the summer, they boat, water ski, and hike the mountains. In the winter, they snowboard and ski. Lake Tahoe is also known for its strong blizzards.

Lake Tahoe is one of the deepest lakes in the United States. It is 1,645 feet deep.

How 'bout That Dam

The Hoover Dam was built on the Colorado River. It was completed in 1935. It stands on the border of Nevada and Arizona. It blocks the flow of the river so that the water can be used to produce electricity. This electricity is sent to Nevada, Arizona, and Southern California. The dam is 726 feet tall and 1,244 feet long. It has a concrete base that is 660 feet thick—that is as long as two football fields!

Only in the Desert

Nevada gets only about nine inches of rain each year. Any plants or animals that live in the desert must live on very little water. Meet the plants that grow in Nevada's deserts and the animals that live on this dry land:

Bitterbrush

Cactus

Rabbitbrush

Sagebrush

Yucca

The **desert bighorn sheep** can run 30 to 40 miles per hour!

The **pygmy rabbit** weighs only one pound.

The **kangaroo rat** doesn't need to drink water—it gets moisture from food.

The **desert tortoise** burrows 30 feet into the ground during winter.

The **western-banded gecko** eats its skin after it sheds.

Utah

The beauty of Utah is amazing. In southern Utah, there are cliffs, canyons, and natural arches. They are made of brilliant red sandstone. In northern Utah, there are mountains and the Great Salt Lake. Utah has five national parks and many national monuments. Almost three million people live in Utah. Most of them live near Salt Lake City.

Utah Is Home

Brigham Young

Utah is home to many people. A thousand years ago, the Anasazi lived in houses that they built into the cliffs. The Fremont people lived in pit houses that were built into the earth. Later, the Navajo, Ute, and Shoshone began to live in this area. In 1847, Brigham Young came to Utah with his Mormon followers. They settled near the Great Salt Lake. They wanted a place to live where they could practice their religion. Today, people from many faiths and backgrounds live in Utah. Some people work for the government. Utah's most valuable product is oil.

Salt Lake Temple

STATE FACTS

Statehood: January 4, 1896—45th state
Capital: Salt Lake City
Nickname: The Beehive State
Motto: Industry
State Bird: California seagull

State Flower: Sego lily
State Animal: Rocky Mountain elk
State Fruit: Cherry
State Insect: Honeybee
State Tree: Blue spruce
State Mineral: Copper
State Fossil: *Allosaurus*
State Vegetable: Spanish sweet onion

The Golden Spike

In the mid-1800s, people began traveling across the country. The Union Pacific Railroad started a railroad in Omaha, Nebraska. It built tracks going west. The Central Pacific Railroad started laying tracks in Sacramento, California. Their tracks went east. On May 10, 1869, the two tracks met at Promontory Point, Utah. They were nailed together with a Golden Spike.

A Rainbow Bridge

Rainbow Bridge National Monument is one of Utah's hidden treasures. It is the largest known natural bridge in the world. The distance from the bottom to the top of the arch is 290 feet. That's nearly the height of the Statue of Liberty. The top of the arch is 42 feet thick. It is 33 feet wide. Rainbow Bridge is sacred to the American Indians in Utah. There is no road to Rainbow Bridge. To get there, people must hike to it.

A State for Parks

Utah has five national parks:

Arches National Park

Bryce Canyon National Park

Canyonlands National Park

Capitol Reef National Park

Zion National Park

If you go to Bryce Canyon National Park, look for the thin spires of rock. They are called "hoodoos" or "fairy chimneys."

A Salty Lake

The Great Salt Lake is in northern Utah. The lake's water is very salty. No fish are able to live in the lake. The tiny brine shrimp are the only animals that can survive here. Four rivers flow into the Great Salt Lake. But no water flows out. If you swim in the lake, be ready for a surprise. The salt in the water makes it easier to float!

DID YOU KNOW?

Land speed races are held at the Bonneville Salt Flats in Utah every year. Racecars reach speeds of more than 400 miles per hour.

Wyoming

Wyoming has fewer people than any other state. About 12,000 years ago, Native Americans lived on this land. About 200 years ago, fur trappers and traders set up trading posts. Travelers on the Oregon Trail passed through Wyoming. Later, ranchers raised large herds of cattle. Today, ranchers still raise cattle. Wyoming also mines more coal than anywhere else in the United States.

Blowing Steam!

Bubbling mud pots, spraying geysers, hissing steam vents—these are just a few of the sights and sounds of Yellowstone National Park. It has 300 geysers. The most famous geyser is called Old Faithful. It blows hot water and steam every 76 minutes! Yellowstone is home to elk, bison, deer, bighorn sheep, pronghorn antelope, and moose. Wolves also live at Yellowstone. This is the oldest national park in the United States. It was created in 1872.

Equal Rights for Women

Wyoming's motto is "Equal Rights." Women have been voting in Wyoming since 1869. This right was given to women when Wyoming was still a territory. In 1870, Esther Morris became a judge in South Pass City. She was the first female judge in the United States. There is a statue of her at the capitol in Cheyenne. There is also another statue of her at the United States Capitol in Washington, D.C.

STATE FACTS

Statehood: July 10, 1890—44th state
Capital: Cheyenne
Nickname: The Equality State
Motto: Equal Rights
State Bird: Meadowlark

State Flower: Indian paintbrush
State Mammal: Bison
State Reptile: Horned toad
State Tree: Plains cottonwood

DID YOU KNOW?

There are more than 25 cities in the country with more people than the whole state of Wyoming.

Buffalo Bill

Wyoming keeps the American West spirit alive at the Buffalo Bill Historical Center. This museum tells the story of William F. "Buffalo Bill" Cody. He was a guide, scout, frontiersman, showman, and actor. He worked to teach people about the American West. The town of Cody, Wyoming, is named after him.

Let's Rodeo!

Rodeo is the state sport of Wyoming. Cowboys and cowgirls compete in many events. Most rodeos have bareback riding, saddle bronco riding, steer wrestling, team roping, tie-down roping, and barrel racing. The Frontier Days Rodeo is held every summer in Cheyenne. It is one of the biggest rodeos in the United States. Smaller rodeos are held in other Wyoming towns all summer long. High school and college students also compete in rodeos. Even kids enjoy the sport. They compete at 4-H and Little Britches rodeos.

Devils Tower

Devils Tower is 1,267 feet high. The steep sides have long grooves. Legend has it that a bear's claws made the grooves. Climbers from all over the world climb Devils Tower. Many choose not to climb it during June to show respect to the Native Americans who believe that Devils Tower is sacred. Devils Tower is in eastern Wyoming. It is near the town of Sundance.

FUN FACT Prairie falcons sometimes make nests in the cracks of Devils Tower. The climbing routes near the nests are closed until the young falcons learn to fly.

Pacific

The Pacific region is very large. Each state is different. Hawaii has warm beaches. Alaska has lots of snow. California has deserts and high mountains. Washington and Oregon have green forests and ranch land. But all of these states have something in common too. Each state touches the Pacific Ocean.

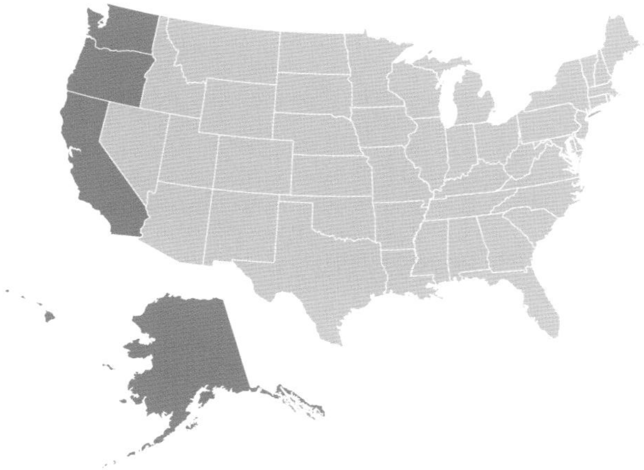

Olympia
WASHINGTON
Salem
OREGON
Honolulu
HAWAII
Sacramento
ALASKA
CALIFORNIA
Juneau

Alaska

California

Hawaii

Oregon

Washington

Kilauea volcano, Hawaii

Active Land

The land in the Pacific region is active. Each state has volcanoes. Mount St. Helens is in southern Washington. It erupted on May 18, 1980. Kilauea is a volcano in Hawaii. Hot lava flowed down this mountain in 2010. Many earthquakes and construction have made the land tremble in the Pacific region. The biggest earthquake in the United States happened in Alaska in 1964.

First People

Thousands of years ago, people crossed over to North America from Asia. Some of the people settled in the land that is now Alaska. Others kept traveling south. They built villages in Washington, Oregon, and California. Many Native Americans still live in the states of the Pacific region. Native people also live on the island of Hawaii. Their ancestors came from other islands in the Pacific Ocean.

Let's Eat!

The states in the Pacific region grow a lot of crops. Large farms in California grow nuts, vegetables, sweet potatoes, melons, strawberries, and all kinds of fruits. Farmers in Washington and Oregon grow apples, pears, plums, potatoes, and wheat. Most Christmas trees come from Oregon. Hawaii has fields of pineapples. People from Alaska fish in the ocean. Fishers catch salmon, herring, and crabs.

Rain or Shine

The weather near the Pacific region is both rainy and sunny. Hoh National Forest is a rainforest in Washington. It gets about 140 inches of rain every year. Hilo, Hawaii, is the wettest city in the United States. Each year, it gets 130 inches of rain. San Francisco, California, gets another kind of moisture. It is called fog. In Centralia, Washington, it is said that it once rained for 55 days in a row! But it's not always rainy in this region. Southern California and Hawaii are known for great sunny weather most of the year.

Alaska

Alaska is the state with the most land. It is two and a half times bigger than Texas. The first Alaskans crossed over from Asia. They were the ancestors of the Inuits, Aleuts, and other Native Americans who live in Alaska today. Alaska is also home to oil field workers and members of the Air Force and Navy. People who want outdoor adventure come to Alaska.

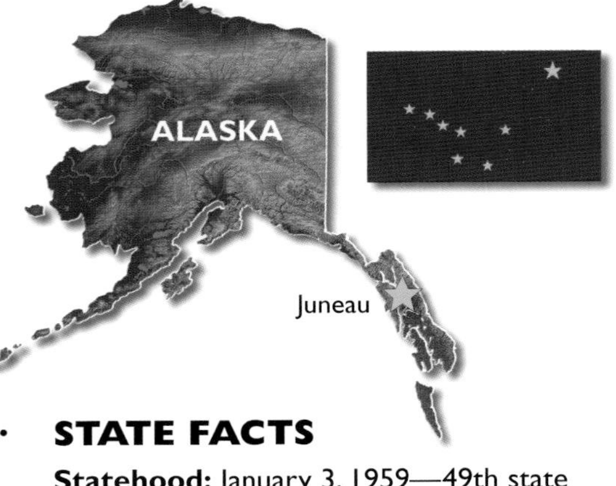

STATE FACTS

Statehood: January 3, 1959—49th state

Capital: Juneau

Nickname: The Last Frontier; or Land of the Midnight Sun

Motto: North to the Future

State Bird: Willow ptarmigan

State Flower: Forget-me-not

State Tree: Sitka spruce

State Fish: King salmon

State Sport: Dog mushing

Anchorage is the largest city in Alaska.

DID YOU KNOW?

The name Alaska comes from the Eskimo word *alakshak*, which means "great land."

Is Alaska an Icebox?

America paid the Russians $7.2 million for all of Alaska in 1867. People laughed when the United States bought this land. They thought Alaska was just a giant "icebox." But then Alaska's riches were found. Not only did Alaska have furs, fish, and whales, but also gas, gold, copper, and coal. In the 1950s and 1960s, people found oil in Alaska. Large amounts of oil sit underground in Prudhoe Bay on the state's north shore. Alaska is still rich in oil today. It is also rich in beauty. Alaska has more wildlife and wilderness than anywhere else in the United States. Alaska became a state in 1959.

Who Drew Alaska's Flag?

Alaska's flag is a deep blue. Yellow stars show the Big Dipper and the North Star. A 13-year-old boy drew the flag in 1926. He was an orphan named Benny Benson. He was part Aleutian and part Russian and lived in Seward, Alaska. His flag was chosen to be the flag of the Alaskan Territory. When Alaska became a state in 1959, the people voted to keep Benny's flag. Today, the flag flies over the Alaska's capitol.

Extreme State!

Not only is Alaska the biggest state, but it also has big facts:

- Tallest mountain in United States: Mount McKinley is 20,320 feet.
- Largest national park: Denali National Park is almost 9,500 square miles.
- Most islands of any state: Alaska has 1,800 named islands.
- Longest state from east to west: Alaska is about 2,400 miles wide. (This is about the same distance as it is from California to Florida!)

Mount McKinley

FUN FACT Alaska has 39 mountain ranges, more than 3 million lakes, and more than 100,000 glaciers. There's only one word to describe it: Wow!

Dog Mushing

The Iditarod is a dog sled race that runs through the Alaskan wilderness. The race is more than 1,150 miles long. It begins in Anchorage and ends in Nome. The race lasts 10 to 17 days. Only the best-trained dogs and "mushers" are able to finish. Long ago, dogsledding was the only way to travel over land in the winter in Alaska. The Iditarod is an important trail. The Iditarod race helps people remember the history of Alaska.

Animals of Alaska

Alaska has many animals. But it has no snakes or other reptiles. It is just too cold for them! Here are some animals that live in the Alaskan cold:

Wolf

Bald Eagle

Caribou

Grizzly Bear

Moose

Otter

California

Sandy beaches. Rocky cliffs. Snowy mountain peaks. Hot deserts. Tall waterfalls and forests. California has all of these natural wonders. California is the third-largest state, but has more people than any other state. Almost 37 million people live in California. Some of the largest cities in the United States are in California near the Pacific Ocean. They are Los Angeles, San Diego, San Francisco, and San Jose.

Golden State History

Native Americans were the first people to live in California. In the 1500s, Spanish explorers began visiting the coast. In 1769, Spanish leaders and priests built missions in the southern part of California. In 1821, Mexico took control of California, but after the Mexican-American War, California became part of the United States. In 1848, a pioneer found gold near Sutter's Mill. The next year people from all over the country rushed to California to search for gold. They are known as the '49ers. California became a state in 1850. Towns and cities grew. California's nickname is the Golden State because of the bright sunshine and the gold rush.

This statue commemorates the gold rush.

STATE FACTS

Statehood: September 9, 1850—31st state
Capital: Sacramento
Nickname: The Golden State
Motto: Eureka (I found it)
State Bird: California valley quail
State Flower: Golden poppy
State Animal: California grizzly bear
State Fish: California golden trout
State Tree: California redwood

DID YOU KNOW?

The oldest living tree on earth is found in Inyo National Forest in California. The bristlecone pines are up to 4,700 years old.

Boats and Rock Art

Long ago, Chumash Indians lived near the Pacific Ocean. They built canoes made of driftwood. They also made boats from the trunks of redwood trees. They often traveled to the Channel Islands. The Chumash people were also artists. They used bright red, orange, and yellow paints to make detailed drawings on sandstone. You can see their rock art at the Painted Cave Historic Park. It is near Santa Barbara, California. People from the Chumash nation still live in California.

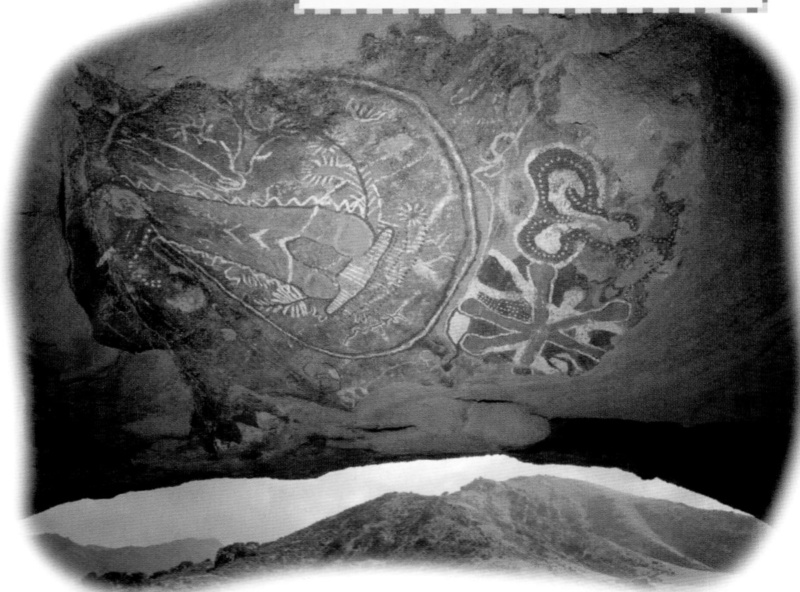

A Golden Bridge

The Golden Gate Bridge is in San Francisco. It is 4,200 feet long and stands more than 270 feet above the water. The bridge was built during the years 1933 to 1937. A safety net was hung below the workers to catch them if they fell. Sadly, 11 people died while building the bridge. Today, ironworkers and painters climb the bridge to do repairs. If you visit San Francisco, you can walk across the Golden Gate Bridge. The sidewalk is 1.7 miles long.

FUN FACT The steel used in the bridge was made in New Jersey, Maryland, and Pennsylvania. It was shipped to California through the Panama Canal.

California by the Numbers

- The tallest tree in America is 368 feet high and lives in Redwood National Park in California. 
- California is the third largest state. 
- California has 8,000 lakes. 
- California's coastline is 840 miles long.
- Yosemite Falls is 2,425 feet tall—it has three separate waterfalls!
- On July 10, 1913, the temperature in Death Valley was 134 degrees.
- Mount Whitney is 14,494 feet tall and is California's highest peak.  
- There are about 1,800,000 dairy cows in California.

Who Was John Muir?

John Muir cared about nature. He wanted to protect the mountains and the forests. More than 100 years ago, Muir talked with the leaders of the United States. He urged them to protect the beauty of the land. In 1890, the United States made Yosemite a national park. Muir helped establish other national parks. He is often called "The Father of Our National Park System." He once said, "Do something for the wilderness and make the mountains glad."

Look Up!

If you go to Yosemite National Park, be sure to look up. The cliff of El Capitan is 3,000 feet high. Ribbon Falls is the highest waterfall in North America at 1,612 feet. In winter, the water reflects the glow of the sunset. It looks like it is on fire! More than three million people visit Yosemite National Park each year. It may feel crowded on the main roads and trails. But most of Yosemite is wilderness area. This area has no roads, no people, and no electricity.

Grown in California

The food on your kitchen table may be from California. This state grows half of the fruits and vegetables in the United States. California cows produce more milk and ice cream than any other state. Farms in California grow almonds, head lettuce, grapes, raisins, strawberries, pistachios, olives, and walnuts. That's a lot of food!

General Tree?

The largest tree (in overall size) in the world is the General Sherman Tree. It grows in Sequoia National Park in central California. It is also one of the world's largest living things. Here are the facts:

- **Height:** 274.9 feet—as tall as a 26-story building.
- **Height of first large branch above ground:** 130 feet—as tall as a 12-story building.
- **Trunk width at bottom:** 36.5 feet—as wide as a city street.
- **Age:** 2,700 years old—imagine the stories it could tell!

FUN FACT A "neighbor" of the General Sherman Tree is the General Grant Tree. The real General Sherman and General Grant led the Union Army during the Civil War.

Golden State Heroes

Walt Disney
created Mickey Mouse and other cartoon characters. He opened a studio in Hollywood, California, in the 1940s.

Sally Ride
was the first American woman in space. She went to college at Stanford University in Palo Alto, California.

César Chávez
helped California's farm workers get fair treatment. He also helped them receive more money for their work.

Venus and Serena Williams
are professional tennis players. They grew up in Compton, California.

American Author

John Steinbeck is a famous American author (writer). He was born in Salinas, California. His stories are about the life and struggles of poor farmers in this region. He won the Nobel Prize in 1962. Today, you can visit the National Steinbeck Center in Salinas. The museum offers programs that inspire young writers!

Meet Mr. Rex and Ms. Dinny

Drive down the highway in Cabazon, California, and what will you see? Two giant dinosaur sculptures! The first dinosaur, Ms. Dinny, took 11 years to build in the 1960s. Another dinosaur, Mr. Rex, was added in 1981. Both are huge and can be seen from far away.

DID YOU KNOW?

Death Valley is the hottest, driest place in the United States. Summer temperatures usually reach higher than 115 degrees.

Living on the Fault Line

There is a long fault line in California. A fault line is made of huge plates of rock underground that push up against each other. When the plates move, they cause earthquakes. The San Andreas Fault runs about 810 miles through central California. This fault line caused a big earthquake that shook San Francisco in 1989.

Hawaii

Aloha! Welcome to the land of beaches and volcanoes. Hawaii is made of many islands—132 islands to be exact! The name of the largest island is also Hawaii. People call it the Big Island. The first Hawaiians came to the islands in large canoes. They named the islands after their chief, Hawaii Loa. Today, almost 1.3 million people live on the Hawaiian Islands. The biggest city is Honolulu.

STATE FACTS

Statehood: August 21, 1959—50th state

Capital: Honolulu

Nickname: The Aloha State

Motto: The Life of the Land Is Perpetuated in Righteousness

State Bird: Nene (also called the Hawaiian goose)

State Flower: Native yellow hibiscus

State Fish: Humuhumunukunuku apua'a

State Dance: Hula

State Tree: Kukui tree

Hawaii History

The first Hawaiians came to the islands about 1,600 years ago. At first, the islands had different chiefs. In 1795, King Kamehameha I brought all the islands under his control. About this time, ships from Europe and the United States began to arrive. In 1891, Queen Lili'uokalani was the ruler of Hawaii. She was the first and only queen of the islands. American sugar planters did not want her to lead the country. She was forced to give up her throne. In 1900, the United States made Hawaii a territory, and in 1959, Hawaii became the 50th state—the last state to join the Union.

DID YOU KNOW?

Mount Waialeale on the island of Kauai gets 460 inches of rain each year!

Pearl Harbor

Pearl Harbor is a large harbor on the island of Oahu. The United States Navy has bases and ships here. On December 7, 1941, the Japanese attacked Pearl Harbor. They destroyed many U.S. Navy ships. This was a surprise attack. The next day the United States entered World War II. You can visit Pearl Harbor today. The USS *Arizona* Memorial honors those who died in the attack.

Surfing is a popular sport in Hawaii.

Red ohia is the flower of the Big Island.

Island Flowers

The state flower of Hawaii is the yellow hibiscus. Each island also has its own flower. The flowers of Kauai and Niihau are not actually flowers, but they are just as beautiful.

Oahu: Yellow ilima

Big Island (Hawaii): Red ohia

Kauai: Mokihana *(This is a green berry grown on Mount Waialelae.)*

Maui: Pink lokelani

Molokai: White kukui blossom

Lanai: Kaunaoa

Niihau: White pupu shell

Kahoolawe: Hinahina

Speak Hawaiian

Most Hawaiians speak English, but they also use Hawaiian words.

Hawaiian word:	How to say it:	What it means:
ae	eye	yes
aloha	ah-LOH-hah	love, hello, good-bye
aole	ah-OH-lay	no
kaukau	KOW-kow	food
luau	LOO-ow	feast
mahalo	mah-HAH-loh	thanks

Volcanoes at Work

The state of Hawaii is made of 132 islands. These islands are actually the tops of mountains that rise up from the bottom of the ocean. Volcanoes formed the islands. Each time the volcanoes erupted, lava flowed out and then cooled, making the islands bigger. Two volcanoes in Hawaii are still active. Both of them are on the Big Island. Mount Kilauea has been spewing lava since 1983. Mauna Loa is the other active volcano. It has not erupted since 1984.

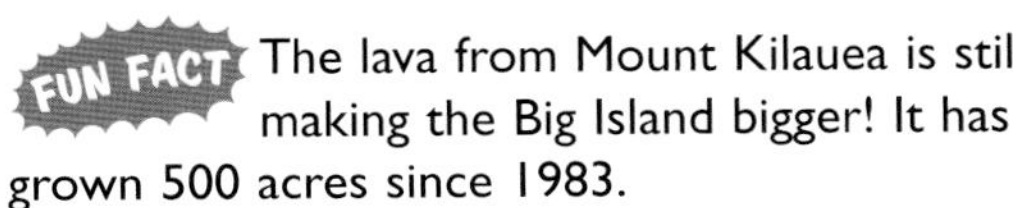

The lava from Mount Kilauea is still making the Big Island bigger! It has grown 500 acres since 1983.

Oregon

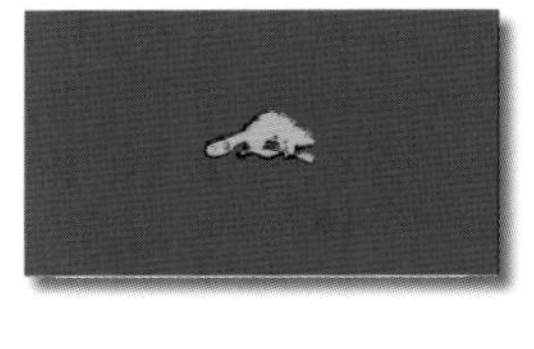

The Cascade Mountains of Oregon run through the middle of the state. The land east of the Cascades is dry with hot summers and cold, sunny winters. Ranchers here raise beef cattle on the open land. West of the Cascades there are forests of fir trees that cover the sides of the hills. Heavy rains fall in this area. Oregon has beautiful beaches along the Pacific coast. Large rocks rise up from the sand to meet the ocean.

Moving to Oregon!

At first, Native Americans lived on the land that is now Oregon. The Chinook, Nez Percé, and Klamath called the Pacific Northwest their home. Explorers from Spain came in the 1500s. They were fur traders, and they hunted beaver. By the mid-1800s, settlers from the East followed the Oregon Trail. They were happy to find good land. Nine different Native American nations still live in Oregon. And more people are moving to Oregon today. Farmers here grow hazelnuts, mint, and flowers for greenhouses. People work in factories making computer and electronic products.

Farmers in Oregon grow mint to make peppermint oil, and this oil is used to make candy canes!

STATE FACTS

Statehood: February 14, 1859—33rd state
Capital: Salem
Nickname: The Beaver State
Motto: She Flies With Her Own Wings
State Bird: Western meadowlark

State Flower: Oregon grape
State Animal: American beaver
State Fish: Chinook salmon

DID YOU KNOW?

Eugene, Oregon, was the first city to have one-way streets.

The Oregon Trail

In the 1840s and '50s, pioneers headed to Oregon Territory. Many of them wanted land. The Oregon Trail was the main land route to the Pacific Northwest. It was 2,170 miles long and ran from Independence, Missouri, to Willamette Valley, Oregon. The trip took about six months. Often the kids walked beside the covered wagons as they traveled. If you go to Baker City, Oregon, you can still see the ruts in the ground that were made from the wheels of these wagons.

Sea Lion Caves

Oregon has some of the largest sea caves in the world. Along Oregon's Pacific coast, north of Florence, are the Sea Lion Caves. Hundreds of sea lions, seals, and many types of sea birds live in these caves. The sea lions also take off from here and swim north to Alaska each winter.

Volcano Lake

Crater Lake is the deepest lake in the United States. It is in the southern part of Oregon. Here's how it formed: 7,700 years ago a volcano stood at this spot. When it erupted, the top of the volcano collapsed. A "caldera" is the hole that forms when a volcano collapses. Only a hole was left. Rain began to fill the hole. Slowly a lake formed. It is called Crater Lake, and it is 1,943 feet deep. Sometimes yellow swirls are seen on the lake. This is pollen from the pine trees.

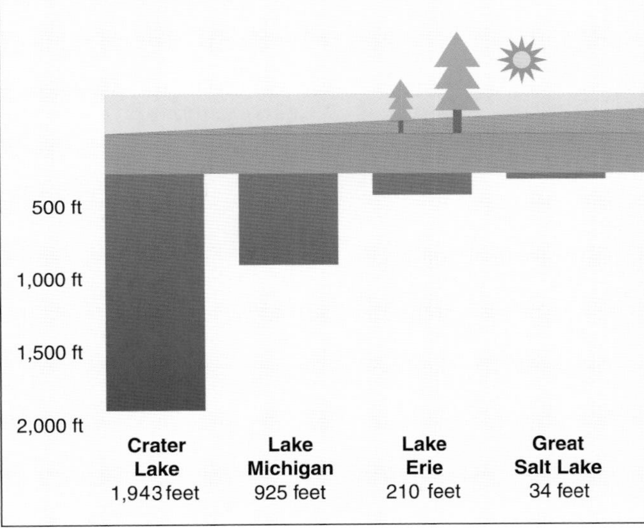

Author from Oregon

Have you read books about Ramona and Beezus? Beverly Cleary wrote them. She was born in McMinnville, Oregon. She grew up in Yamhill and Portland. Her stories often take place in the neighborhood where she lived. If you go to Portland, you can see statues of Henry Huggins, Ramona, and Ribsy. They are four blocks away from the real Klickitat Street, where her characters live.

Washington

The state of Washington is named after George Washington. It is the only state that is named after a president. Its nickname is the Evergreen State. Forests of pine trees and fir trees grow all over the land and mountains. The Columbia River forms part of the border between Washington and Oregon. The Pacific Ocean lies to the west. Washington has some tall mountains. Mount Rainier of the Cascade Mountains is 14,410 feet high.

STATE FACTS

Statehood: November 11, 1889—42nd state

Capital: Olympia

Nickname: The Evergreen State

Motto: Alki (By and By)

State Bird: Willow goldfinch

State Flower: Coast rhododendron

State Marine Mammal: Orca

State Fruit: Apple

State Fish: Steelhead trout

State Tree: Western hemlock

State Vegetable: Walla Walla sweet onion

Who Gets Washington?

During the 1800s, American and British settlers lived in the Oregon Territory that would become Washington. Which country would get the land? The two countries did not have a war. Instead, they decided on a border. The British leaders gave the United States the land south of the border. Today, this is the border between Washington and Canada.

A Wet Sound

Can a "sound" be water? Yes! A sound is a part of the ocean that is between two pieces of land. The Puget Sound is in the northwest part of Washington. Most of Washington's large cities are near Puget Sound. Seattle and Tacoma are two of these cities. Many boats and ships travel across Puget Sound. Ferry-boats take people from the islands to Seattle. Cargo ships move goods to other ports—sometimes, they go all the way to Asia! Cruise ships also travel across Puget Sound. They take people on vacation from Seattle to Canada and Alaska.

DID YOU KNOW?

In 1986, Mount Mitchell had more than 14 inches of rain in one day!

What Lives in Puget Sound?

The Puget Sound is full of life.

Orca whales often swim in pods (groups).

Harbor seals like to sleep on beaches and rocks.

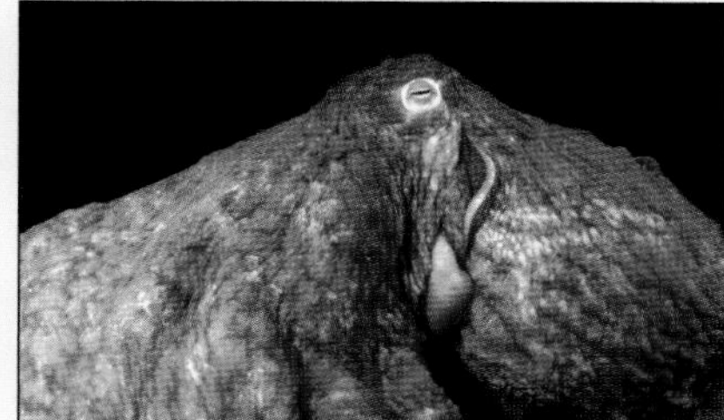

Giant Pacific Octopi are the largest octopi in the world.

Sixgill sharks grow to be 14 feet long.

Wolf eels have faces that are hard to forget.

An Apple a Day

Washington grows more apples than any other state. This state grows about 130 million bushels of apples each year. Most apples are grown in orchards in central Washington. Red Delicious and Gala are the most popular kinds of apples. Washington also grows other crops. Wheat is grown on the rolling hills in the southeast part of the state. Walla Walla sweet onions are grown in this area too.

Mount St. Helens Erupts

Mount St. Helens is a volcano in the Cascade Range. It had been inactive since 1857. But in 1980, Mount St. Helens erupted. The volcano shot ash and rocks into the sky and over a huge area. The eruption knocked down trees and started forest fires. It melted mountain snow, which created floods. Ash from the volcano threatened crops and wildlife as well as people and homes in nearby towns. It took years for greenery on the mountain to start growing back.

The Cascade Range has four more major volcanoes. They are Mount Baker, Glacier Peak, Mount Rainier, and Mount Adams.

Index